WILLS FOR BRITISH COLUMBIA

WILLS FOR BRITISH COLUMBIA

Steven G. Wong, B.Sc., LL.B.

Self-Counsel Press
(*a division of*)
International Self-Counsel Press Ltd.
Canada   USA

Self-Counsel Press acknowledges the financial support of the Government of Canada through the Book Publishing Industry Development Program (BPID) for our publishing activities.

Printed in Canada

First edition: 1972
Tenth edition: 1985
Fifteenth edition: 1991
Sixteenth edition: 1993
Reprinted: 1993, 1994
Seventeenth edition: 1995
Reprinted: 1995, 1996 (2)
Eighteenth edition: 1997
Reprinted: 1998, 1999
Nineteenth edition: 2000
Reprinted: 2001

Canadian Cataloguing in Publication Data

Wong, Steven G., 1943 -
    Wills for British Columbia
    (Self-counsel legal series)
    ISBN 1-55180-326-7

    1. Wills — British Columbia — Popular works.
2. Probate law and practice — British Columbia — Popular works.
I. Title. II. Series.
KEB245.Z82W66 2000   346.71105'4   C00-911076-3
KF755.Z9W66 2000

Self-Counsel Press
(a division of)
International Self-Counsel Press Ltd.
1481 Charlotte Road
North Vancouver, BC   V7J 1H1

1704 N. State Street
Bellingham, WA 98225

ORDER FORM

To: Self-Counsel Press
        1481 Charlotte Road
        North Vancouver, B.C.
        V7J 1H1

Please send me —

_____Have You Made Your Will? (with disk) Kit,
        $11.95

Please add $3.50 postage to your order and PST and GST to the total.

All prices subject to change without notice.

❑ Money order enclosed for $_____.
❑ Charge to my credit card (see below).

Name _____

Address _____

City _____ Province _____

Postal code _____Telephone_____

MasterCard/Visa number:_____

Expiry date:_____ Validation date _____

Signature:_____

CONTENTS

LIST OF SAMPLES

NOTICE TO READERS

Laws are constantly changing. Every effort is made to keep this publication as current as possible. However, the author, the publisher and the vendor of this book make no representation or warranties regarding the outcome or the use to which the information in this book is put and are not assuming any liability for any claims, losses, or damages arising out of the use of this book. The reader should not rely on the author or publisher of this book for any professional advice. Please be sure that you have the most recent edition.

Note: The fees quoted in this book are correct at the date of publication. However, fees are subject to change without notice. For current fees, please check with the appropriate government office nearest you.

FOREWORD

The making of a will is unquestionably one of the most important things you will do in your lifetime. No price can be placed on the peace of mind that results from the knowledge that clear, legally valid instructions govern the disposition of your worldly goods. Those who mourn your death may not be pleased with the dispositions you make, but at least there is less chance of a family-splitting lawsuit if the will has been properly drawn.

Even though every legal system in the world has rules about the disposition of the property, goods, and wealth of a person who dies without a will, dispositions in accordance with rules are seldom as satisfactory as those made in accordance with the deceased's wishes as expressed in a properly drawn and signed will. The solution is simple. Everyone should make a will on reaching the age when it is legal to do so and should revise or review it every two or three years.

The purpose of this book is to tell you in non-legal terms how to make a will. It shows how you can legally prepare your own will and, more important, it shows you how you can save time in preparing your will. There is a lot more to the making of even the simplest will than is generally known. This book attempts to explain some of the whys and hows. It is written by a lawyer who is the first to admit that it will not answer all the questions that may arise when making a will. But it is not intended to be more than a guide that explains the rules and the problems with suggestions for their possible solutions. It also defines some of the legal complications that may arise for the relatives and friends of those who die without leaving a proper will.

— *The Editors*

1

INTRODUCTION TO WILLS
AND LAWYERS

a. WHAT IS A WILL?

A will is a document containing a set of instructions that become effective upon the death of the person who made the will. If the person making a will is a man, he is referred to as a testator; a woman who makes a will is called a testatrix. A will directs how the possessions of the deceased are to be divided among the persons named as beneficiaries in the will.

Your will covers all of your assets located anywhere in the world (unless you specifically restrict it to assets located in the province in which you are residing). If you have assets in another country, you should consult a lawyer specializing in wills.

Generally the will authorizes a man (called an executor) or a woman (called an executrix) to collect assets, pay off debts, and divide the property according to the wishes of the deceased as stated in the will. (In this book, all references to a testator or executor also apply to a testatrix or executrix and vice versa.) (**Note:** Do not confuse a will with a power of attorney. A will takes effect when a person dies; a power of attorney ceases when the grantor dies. See the Glossary for definition. Also refer to Self-Counsel's *Power of Attorney Kit* for more information.)

b. DO YOU NEED A LAWYER?

It is not always necessary to retain a lawyer to make a will, but people in any one of the following categories should get legal advice.

1. People who are about to be married

There have been more than a few tragic accidents during honeymoons, with resulting legal complications.

2. Owners of large, complex estates

People in this category should consult lawyers, especially if they hold shares in international, public, and private companies, or real estate holdings. A competent lawyer not only helps ensure the proper disposition of these estates, he or she also helps secure whatever tax benefits may be available.

3. People who are very old or who suffer from mental or physical disabilities

Those who have histories of mental disorders or who may lapse into periods of semi-consciousness should have their wills drawn by lawyers. If they do not, their wills may be challenged or set aside on the grounds that they were insane, did not understand what they were signing, or were otherwise incompetent at the time of making their wills.

4. Infants (anyone in British Columbia under the age of 19)

These people cannot make their own wills because they have no legal capacity to do so. There are, however, two exceptions:

(a) An infant who is married, or has been married, may legally make a will even though he or she has not reached the age of 19.

(b) An infant who is under 19 but a member of the armed forces on active duty may legally make a will. This is also true of sailors while in the course of a voyage.

5. People who are separated or about to be divorced

The danger here is that the estate of a separated person may go to his or her spouse under the law. A lawyer's advice is necessary to ensure that any property is properly protected and legally passes to the desired beneficiaries.

The Family Relations Act provides that property owned by either spouse (even if registered in a spouse's sole name) may be a "family asset" if the asset is used by both spouses or if the non-titled spouse (i.e., the person who is not the registered owner) has made any contribution in time, in money, or in efforts to acquire or maintain the "family asset." If, for example, you have a house (in which you and your spouse have lived) in your own name, then your spouse could legally claim up to one-half of the house. (In some circumstances, a greater share could be claimed where maintenance is awarded.) Obviously, if by operation of law your spouse receives half of your property, you would not be able to "will" that property to your children, friend, or relations.

In the absence of a property agreement with your spouse, if you separate, you could each claim one-half of the other's property. Therefore, if you are separated, about to be separated, or about to be divorced, you should have your will drawn by a lawyer.

One significant section in the Wills Act provides that if a person is divorced or has a court-ordered separation, his or her will is to be interpreted as though the spouse had died first. This means that any gift to the spouse or an appointment of a spouse as executor or trustee will be revoked under these circumstances. Therefore, you should see a lawyer and amend your will if you are or anticipate being divorced.

If you are simply separated, but not yet divorced, and you want your spouse to be executor and trustee because the estate is going to your children and your spouse is guardian, state the following in your will:

3

This will is made in anticipation of possible divorce and should remain the same upon divorce.

6. People born or married under a community property system

People who were born or married in Quebec or a state such as Washington may have certain restrictions placed on what they can dispose of in their wills, and to whom they can give it. In such a jurisdiction, a married person's interest in his or her spouse's property may be forfeited by means of a legally drawn-up pre- or post-nuptial settlement agreement.

7. People living in common-law relationships

The rights of people living common-law are unclear, and legal advice is recommended for common-law spouses making a will. Various statutes define a common-law relationship differently. For example, the Estate Administration Act defines it as "a person who has lived and cohabited with another person as a spouse and has been maintained by that other person for a period of not less than two years immediately preceding his death."

For Canada Pension death benefits an applicant need only show that the couple resided together as husband and wife for at least one year and that the deceased publicly represented the applicant as his or her spouse.

A common-law spouse must apply to the courts to obtain a share of the estate if there is no will, and the share is at the discretion of the courts. Further, a common-law spouse must request the Minister of Health and Welfare Canada to exercise his discretion in granting survivor's benefits.

8. People who have beneficiaries with mental or major physical disabilities

If a beneficiary is unable to handle his or her own affairs, the courts may appoint someone to oversee this duty. This individual could be a total stranger to your family. Seek legal advice if you want to avoid this.

9. People who have a child or children born out of wedlock, but are not maintaining them

A child born out of wedlock may still have a claim against the non-supporting parent under the Wills Variation Act.

c. HOW MUCH WILL A LAWYER CHARGE?

A lawyer's fee for a simple will is usually around $100, but in the case of people with more complicated estates or special problems, the cost may be substantially higher.

If you fall within any of the categories noted in section **b.**, and particularly if you own a large, complicated estate, you would be wise to seek legal advice and expect to pay more than the fee quoted above. In the more complicated situations, lawyers may charge a set amount per hour, or they may quote a fixed fee for the complete preparation of the will. In any case, the peace of mind that accompanies the knowledge that the document is properly drawn and signed is an important consideration that cannot be reduced to monetary terms.

d. WHY SHOULD YOU MAKE A WILL?

If you make a will, you can assure yourself that your possessions will be distributed according to your wishes when you die. An even more important consideration is that if you die with no will (i.e., intestate) or without proper provisions for an executor, there will be delays in processing your estate that may create hardship for your family, friends, and business associates.

No matter how small or large you estimate your estate to be, it is very important that you make a will. A properly drawn will saves those who survive you immeasurable time, money, energy, and emotional stress. Remember to revise your will from time to time throughout your life and make sure that your executor or lawyer always knows where to find your will and your list of assets.

e. WHAT HAPPENS IF YOU DIE WITHOUT A WILL?

If you die intestate (without having made a legally valid will) someone, usually one of your next-of-kin, must apply to the court to be appointed as an administrator of the estate. If no decision can be made about which particular individual should be appointed administrator, two or more joint administrators can apply, or the public trustee can be appointed administrator. If you have to involve the public trustee, be prepared for a long wait as that office is usually very busy.

The appointment of an administrator can be complicated and time-consuming, especially if the next-of-kin live in distant parts of the country or in another country. In addition, in cases in which children are to receive part of the estate, the courts require that the administrator post a bond before he or she can be appointed. This bond can be for as much as twice the value of the assets held in trust for the children, but is normally for just an equivalent value. To give you an idea of the cost of being bonded, a bond of $100 000 will have an annual premium of about $310 per year. This can amount to quite a sum. For example, if a widow has two children, aged three and six, with funds held in trust for each of them, she will end up paying premiums until the youngest child reaches the age of majority at 19. However, if the widow is given the function of administering the funds for the children under the terms of the will, she does not have to be bonded.

A will can empower a widow to use some or all of the capital held in trust for her children at her own discretion. If no will is left, the widow is forced to apply for a court order every time she wants to spend some of the capital in the trust fund.

If you fail to make a will, your children may not be placed in the custody of a person whom you would like. Disagreements over who will look after the children can be messy, expensive, and heartbreaking.

The Estate Administration Act governs the disposition of a deceased person's property if there is no will. However, if a piece of real estate is registered in joint tenancy, the real estate passes to the surviving joint tenant. No will is needed because the property passes automatically because of the right of survivorship. The property held in joint tenancy does not "fall into the estate."

If the surviving spouse does not receive the matrimonial home by law, as in a joint tenancy or under the provisions of a will, problems can arise. For example, the provisions of the Estate Administration Act entitle the widow or widower to remain in the home for life (even if the home is of far greater value than $65 000, which is the surviving spouse's preference share under the Estate Administration Act).

The widow or widower is entitled to remain in the family home for life and owns all of the household furnishings. The house may not be sold until the spouse dies or agrees to the sale and gives up his or her life interest in the family home. As the provision regarding the surviving spouse's right to the use of the family home comes before the rights of the children to their portions of the estate, all of the major assets of the deceased's estate may be tied up and unable to be distributed to adult children until the surviving spouse consents to the sale of the property.

If a will directed the distribution of the assets, the home could be transferred directly to the surviving spouse or to adult children without any of the problems caused by these provisions of the Estate Administration Act.

If a person dies intestate leaving no widow, widower, children, or other relative, the Crown (i.e., the provincial government) takes the estate by virtue of "escheats." This simply means that, because there is no one to inherit, the Crown takes possession of all the property. Thus, if you have no spouse or other known relative and you do not want the provincial government to possess whatever you own when you die, you must make a will.

See chapter 4 for more particulars.

f. EUTHANASIA AND THE "LIVING WILL"

Advances in medical science have enabled doctors to keep humans "alive" while, in fact, the person involved may be totally reliant on extraordinary artificial means of life support, such as medical machines. Euthanasia ("painless death") is a sensitive subject among members of the medical profession. This is not hard to understand as traditionally the purpose of a doctor (as en-shrined by the Hippocratic oath) is to extend life, not to end it. However, attitudes are changing, and for those who are concerned with the quality of life when near death, information on the "living will" is included here for consideration.

It should be noted that the "living will" is actually a misnomer, as a true will takes effect only upon the death of the person making the will. A "living will" is, in essence, a declaration of your wishes to the people most likely to have an influence over your care (i.e., your family physician, lawyer, and clergyman).

It should also be noted that those individuals who use a "living will" may create problems for those who abide by the instructions contained in it because it is a criminal offence to terminate a person's life, even in response to his or her request. Theoretically, it would be possible to sustain a charge of criminal negligence if, say, a doctor "forgot" to administer a certain drug or turn on a certain machine. Not only that, if a doctor actively did something to terminate the life of a patient, such as knowingly administering a certain drug that causes death, a charge of murder is possible.

Of course, some doctors are practising euthanasia now, but it is done strictly on an individual basis. You can understand the reluctance of the medical profession to officially

8

approve such practice in view of the provisions of the Criminal Code. The Susan Rodriguez case is an example of the reluctance of the courts to sanction assisted suicide.

If you decide to use a "living will," remember that it has no legal validity, and your doctor and next-of-kin must be prepared to co-operate. Also, don't put the document with your will, which is looked at only after your death. Put it in a place where your relatives can find it and tell them where it is or, better yet, give them copies.

To make best use of your "living will," follow these steps.

(a) Sign and date it before two witnesses. (This helps ensure that you signed of your own free will and not under any pressure.)

(b) Discuss the request with your doctor to make sure that he or she is in agreement. Leave a copy with your doctor for your medical file.

(c) Give copies to those most likely to be concerned "if the time comes when you can no longer take part in decisions for your own future." Enter their names on the bottom line of the "living will." Keep the original nearby, easily and readily available.

(d) Above all, discuss your intentions with those closest to you, now.

(e) It is a good idea to look over your "living will" once a year and redate it and initial the new date to make it clear that your wishes are unchanged.

(f) Ask a lawyer to incorporate the last paragraph of the "living will" in your actual will.
Sample #1 is an example of the preprinted living will form available from the publisher (see page v).

g. REFORM IN GUARDIANSHIP LAW

Four new statutes were enacted on February 28th 2000 relating to adult guardianship:

(a) Adult Guardianship Act

(b) Health Care (Consent) and Care Facility (Admission) Act

(c) Office of the Public Trustee Act

(d) Representation Agreement Act

If a person has a relative or friend that is or might be affected by mental or physical infirmities, then it is recommended that he or she consult a lawyer to ascertain if any of the these laws would assist in alleviating some of his or her concerns.

1. Adult Guardianship Act

Previously, when a person was unable to handle his or her own affairs, someone (usually a relative) had to apply to court to be appointed as a committee. The new act provides for a Needs and Capacity Review to determine what kind of help is needed. The court will decide from three categories:

(a) An *associate decision maker*, who can only assist an adult in making a decision

(b) A *substitute decision maker*, who may be restricted to decisions relating to only certain matters or may be limited to acting for a set time period

(c) A *guardian* who can make all decisions for the adult and is entrusted with ensuring the well-being of the adult.

2. Health Care (Consent) and Care Facility (Admission) Act

When an adult is unable to consent to being admitted to a health care facility, this new law allows a temporary decision maker to be appointed. This person is given authority to decide treatment.

10

2

YOUR WILL

a. THE REQUIREMENTS OF A SENSIBLE, LEGAL WILL

Whether you wish to prepare your own will or have someone else do it for you, you should observe the following basic rules and recommendations.

1. The use of precedents

A will does not have to be written in any set form but it is advisable to follow what is known as a "precedent." This acts as a guide to help you express your intentions clearly in a form that you know has previously met with success.

Several typical precedents that can be easily adapted to your own requirements are shown in Samples #3 to #8. When purchasing a will form, be sure to specify that you want a form that is valid in British Columbia. Self-Counsel Press has a supply of will forms and estate planning kits. (Please refer to the order form at the front of the book.)

2. Put it in writing

The will must be in writing — either handwritten or type-written. (It cannot be tape-recorded for example.) It is preferable to put your will on ordinary letter-size paper (8½ x 11) if you are drawing it up yourself.

3. Include a domicile clause

A "domicile clause" is simply a statement that you are, for example,

John Doe, of Suite 201, 1170 Any Street, City of
Anytown, in the Province of British Columbia.

I recommend that you include a domicile clause in your
will.

4.   Revoke previous wills

It is usual to include a clause revoking all previous wills and
codicils. For example,

I HEREBY REVOKE all previous wills and testamentary dispositions....

5.   Signing the will and having it witnessed

In British Columbia, you, the maker of the will, and the two
witnesses should be 19 years of age or older. In other provinces, all parties should have reached the legal age of majority. (See page 2 for exceptions.)

The will must be signed on the last page by you in the
presence of two witnesses. These witnesses must sign the will
in your presence and in the presence of each other. The two
witnesses together must either see you sign, or see you ac-
knowledge your signature (i.e., say "this is my signature to
my will.") It is essential that the two witnesses do this together.

Great care must be taken with these formalities when the
person making the will is seriously ill. A will has been declared invalid because the testator was too weak to turn over
in bed and the witnesses, in effect, signed the will behind his
back.

It is not a legal requirement, but it is recommended that
each page of the will be initialled by you and by the two
witnesses, all in the presence of each other. This eliminates
the possibility of someone substituting different pages in the
will.

A witness must not be a beneficiary named in the will,
nor should he or she be the spouse of a beneficiary. If the

beneficiary or the beneficiary's spouse witnesses a will, then neither of them can benefit from it. The portion that would have gone to the beneficiary falls into the residual portion of the estate and is distributed in accordance with the "residue clause."

6. Name your personal representative

The will should state who is to be the executor or executrix of the will. An alternative personal representative should also be appointed because if the first executor dies while processing the estate, then an executor named in your executor's will is responsible for processing your estate. Thus you may end up having your estate processed by a stranger unless you provide an alternative.

> I appoint Jean Doe to be the executrix of my will. In the event that Jean Doe is for any reason unable or unwilling to act as executrix hereof or fails to complete the administration of my estate, I appoint John Doe to be the executor of my will.

In all cases, be certain that the executor or executrix you appoint is a person younger than you, so that he or she has a greater chance to survive you. He or she should be a reliable, responsible person. If you are married, your spouse should probably be your executor. This will avoid possible conflict between your spouse and an executor. Of course, if the estate is very large and complicated, or your spouse lacks business sense, you may wish to appoint a business associate as an executor or co-executor. Note also the possible difficulties if you are later divorced from your spouse (see page 3).

7. The 30-day clause

One of the most important clauses to be included in your will is what is known as the "30-day clause". This applies even if both you and your spouse have made wills. If both of you were killed in the same accident and left wills leaving everything to each other, the estate would be faced with a situation similar to an intestacy (no will). If your only beneficiary (your spouse) dies after you do leaving his or her estate to you, then there are no named beneficiaries surviving and an administrator would have to be appointed for your spouses's estate, the consents of the next-of-kin obtained and, perhaps, bonds posted. Your property would then be distributed by operation of law and not according to your wishes. The 30-day clause is shown in the precedents in Samples #3 to #5, but to help you, I explain it here in greater detail.

The reason for the 30-day time period is that statistics indicate that if a person survives an accident for that length of time, he or she usually recovers. Keep in mind that you don't want a delay that is too lengthy before your will takes effect. For example, if your wife is an executrix as well as a beneficiary and a 30-day clause is used in the appointment, she will not be able to apply for Letters Probate until that time limit has expired. It is better to keep the appointment in a separate clause to avoid causing delay in the process of the estate.

The 30-day clause should offer an alternative recipient for a bequest and should read as follows:

> To my wife, Jean Doe, should she survive me for 30 days, I give, devise and bequeath my house and car. If she fails to survive me for 30 days, then the house and car to my son, John Doe.

Note: If both husband and wife die in the same accident, it is presumed by law that the younger spouse survived the older. Assume, as is usually the case, that the husband leaves his belongings to his wife who is younger, then the wife is believed to be the beneficiary of her spouse's property even if she owns the property for only one minute or less.

You should be aware that many preprinted will forms purchased at stationery stores do not contain some of these clauses, particularly the 30-day clause. If you intend to use preprinted will forms, it is recommended that you do so in conjunction with this book, and that you put your signature next to any deletions, and have your two witnesses initial the information that you write or type in.

8. Appoint a guardian

If both you and your spouse are making a will and have young children, it is very important that you consider who should be a guardian if both of you are killed. Usually the worst people to select are your parents because of the age gap that could result when your children are 14 or 15 and your parents are in their seventies and eighties. There is too much risk that they will be too old to be able to do the job. It is better to select a close friend or relative near your own age. Discuss the appointment with the person you select as you may wish to make provisions in the will for a lump sum so the guardian can add on to his or her own home or purchase a new one if it becomes necessary for him or her to assume the position.

9. Read it over

You should read the will over very carefully before signing it to make certain that it is correct in all respects. Be sure that all the beneficiaries are properly identified and their names spelled correctly, especially in situations where there are several close relatives with similar names, or where there is a spouse and children from a previous marriage. Any corrections, deletions, or insertions between the lines must be initialled by you and the two witnesses at the time the changes are made to make them valid. After your death, the court will not approve uninitialled changes and will not permit the dispositions that are affected by the changes to be valid. This law was enacted to prevent people from wrongfully altering the deceased's will for their own benefit.

b. SPECIAL CLAUSES

There are many clauses that may reflect your after-death wishes and that you might like to include in your will. The examples given in this section will assist you in making your decision, but if you are in doubt about any of these clauses and how they relate to your true wishes, consult a lawyer.

1. Life estate

Some people, for whatever reason, may wish to exert control, even after death, over the disposition of a bequest to a surviving spouse if he or she remarries. Such a clause could be worded as follows:

> If my wife, Jean Doe, should survive me for 30 days I give, devise, and bequeath our matrimonial home to her for her use during her lifetime. Upon my said wife's death, then my matrimonial home shall be sold by my trustees and the proceeds divided equally among my children alive at the time of my demise.

2. Encroachment on capital

If you have appointed a trustee to administer your estate and wish to grant to your trustee the right to encroach (spend the capital) or to take needed money out of the amount invested, you may do so.

It is wise to give this power to encroach to the trustees (rather than to the beneficiaries) because the sum involved is not taxed until it is actually received by the beneficiaries. If a sole beneficiary is given the power to encroach upon capital, he or she is taxed by the federal government on the full amount held in the trust on the grounds that all of the capital of the trust could be withdrawn if the beneficiary wished. Whether or not the beneficiary actually withdraws the full amount is irrelevant.

In this case, a clause such as the following may be used:

> I hereby grant to my trustees the right to encroach upon the capital of my estate for funds necessary to maintain and support my spouse and children.

(For more information on trusts, see chapter 5.)

3. Investments

You should give the trustees the power to invest in things other than those covered in the Trustee Act or the Insurance Act, otherwise you may unnecessarily restrict them to low-yield, safe investments and so unnecessarily decrease the value of the estate. The following clause is recommended.

> I hereby grant to my trustees the right to invest in any business or company, at their discretion, even though such investment may not be authorized by the Trustee Act or the Insurance Act.

This clause should be inserted only if you wish to broaden the trustees' powers.

4. Trustee's powers

You may also give the trustees power to handle business affairs and family finances by using the following clause to give them all the powers you would have had if alive.

> I hereby grant to my trustees all the powers that I would have had if I were alive.

Under the law, trustees must be unanimous in their decisions in order to act, but you may wish the majority decision to rule. The following clause will ensure this.

> The majority of the trustees shall decide any matter and their decision shall be binding upon all the trustees and beneficiaries.

If there are only two trustees make one of them senior to the other by using the phrase, "Trustee (name) shall have the deciding vote." This will help avoid deadlocks.

5. Matrimonial home

Sometimes wills include a clause as follows:

> If my wife is living in our matrimonial home at the time of my death, then she may live there as long as she desires.

19

In this case, the direction applies even if the wife would rather live elsewhere. It is better to put in a clause reading:

> My wife may substitute a house or an apartment of equal or lesser value as her residence in place of the matrimonial home or residence in which we are residing at the time of my demise.

You may give trustees or executors yet another power with this clause.

> If one of my trustees or executors predeceases me or is unable or unwilling to act, then the remaining trustee or executor may appoint a new trustee or executor.

This clause transfers your power of appointment to the trustee or executor.

6. Personal property

Personal property ("personalty" in legal terms) is generally given to the spouse. If this is the case, you can avoid itemizing each article by using a "blanket" clause reading:

> Should my spouse survive me for 30 days, I hereby grant to my spouse all my personal property whatsoever and wheresoever situated. If he fails to survive me for 30 days, I grant all my personal property whatsoever and wheresoever situated to Joan Doe.

In cases where a particular article is very valuable, it is wiser to describe it in detail.

> To my son, John, I give my Bulova watch with 25 jewels and gold watch band.

Include in your will a list of items going to a particular beneficiary. If you leave it to the discretion of a trustee, it can cause arguments and hard feelings.

7. Donation of body or organs

Many people want their bodies left wholly or partially for medical research or training. Some wish only certain transplantable organs donated to prolong the life or faculties of someone else. If you wish part or all of your body to be donated for humanitarian purposes, you should make special arrangements well before death. You must sign declarations making it legal for your personal representative to act. Your next-of-kin should also be notified. In addition, you should include a clause in the will like the following:

> I hereby give my eyes to the Eye Bank of Canada under the auspices of the Canadian National Institute for the Blind. I hereby confirm the arrangements made by me during my lifetime respecting this gift of my eyes and instruct my executor to carry out such arrangements upon my death.

It is wise to notify the medical foundation concerned of your arrangements and ensure that they need your remains. Your family physician should also be informed. At all times carry a card in your wallet or purse stating that, in the event of your death, the medical foundation concerned is to be contacted immediately.

At present, various hospitals and universities, such as the University of British Columbia, Faculty of Medicine, require anatomical specimens for teaching purposes.

You may also arrange for the donation of organs through the BC Transplant Society (a sticker on your driver's licence is no longer sufficient). The address details are in Appendix 2.

8. Burial instructions

A clause expressing your wishes on the burial, cremation, or other disposition of your body is recommended. You may also indicate the maximum amount to be spent on your funeral and where interment or cremation should take place. If you choose to be cremated, you may also direct where you want your ashes scattered. The executor has the duty of supervising funeral arrangements, so is empowered to stop your spouse if he or she wants an expensive funeral. If the executor orders a very expensive funeral contrary to the instructions in the will, he or she may be liable for the excess amount. Usually normal burial procedures are followed unless the deceased person expressed otherwise.

9. RRSP

If you have a registered retirement savings plan (RRSP), you may want to mention it specifically in your will. Your contributions to the plan are tax deductible and the income earned from the plan is not taxable. However, when you take money out of the plan, that money is added to your income and taxable for that year.

When a plan holder dies without designating a beneficiary, all funds are paid to the estate and are taxed as if it was income received on the date of death. If you designate your spouse as the beneficiary, then he or she may rollover (transfer the monies to his or her own RRSP) without incurring any tax liabilities. This transfer must take place within 60 days after the end of the year the money is received.

Individuals with significant amounts in their RRSP should be aware of potential tax obligations that result when they name a beneficiary who is not a spouse. This is partly because some RRSP issuers will pay the gross amount of the RRSP to the designated beneficiary without deducting or witholding any tax. If the beneficiary refuses to voluntarily pay the taxes on the monies he or she has received, this may create a dilemma since most wills state that all liabilities (including taxes) are to be paid by the estate. If there are only sufficient funds to pay the taxes and nothing else, then all bequests and gifts will fail (except for the RRSP). If there are insufficient funds to even pay the taxes, it is likely that Revenue Canada will endeavor to collect the taxes from the testator's RRSP proceeds.

You can avoid leaving a beneficiary an unexpected tax bill along with your RRSP by either

(a) stipulating in the RRSP contract that the beneficiary is to receive the proceeds only if he or she agrees to be responsible for the taxes and have the issuer of the plan agree to remit to Revenue Canada at least 30% of the gross proceeds, or

(b) purchasing sufficient life insurance (with the estate as beneficiary) so that adequate funds are available to pay all taxes, or

(c) entering into an agreement with the beneficiary that the beneficiary will pay all income tax liabilities attributed to the RRSP proceeds

You should advise your lawyer or executor if you choose one of these options.

c. SPECIFIC BEQUESTS

If you have a favorite relative to whom you wish to leave a legacy, it is recommended that you state the amount of the gift (e.g., "I give one thousand ($1 000) dollars to John Doe.") If it is a specific item, then describe the item in sufficient detail in the will so that your executor will know exactly what it is you wish to leave to the beneficiary. Here is an example of a clause that will allow you to bequeath specific shares:

> I direct my executor to transfer to Harry Doe my shares in Smokeless Stacks Incorporated. If at my death the said shares as the result of any stock dividend, stock split, amalgamation, reconstruction, or rearrangement of the capital of the said company or the sale of its undertaking to any other company shall be represented by a different capital holding either in the said company or in any other company to which I am entitled at my death, then the said bequest shall take effect as it if had been a bequest of the capital holding or holdings which as the result of such stock dividend, stock split, amalgamation, reconstruction, or rearrangement or sale took the place of such shares.

You may wish to set up a small trust to provide funds to maintain a favorite pet. Of course, you should realize that it would probably be more beneficial to the animal if it were given to someone who would care for it.

It is not recommended that you attempt to make a complicated or foolish bequest. Although foolish bequests may be valid, there is always the danger that they may be found invalid. The usual grounds for challenging foolish bequests is that the testator was of unsound mind and thus incapable of making a valid will. An example of a questionable bequest is one which leaves 90% of your possessions to your pet goldfish. Your next-of-kin would likely start a lawsuit in this case, and the cost of lawyers would be paid out of the estate. This reduces the amount available for distribution to the beneficiaries when all lawsuits are decided.

When setting up trust funds, you should also be alert to the danger posed by the Rule Against Perpetuities. This is a rule of law which invalidates an attempt to set up a trust in which only the interest is paid out indefinitely and the main body of the trust fund is never passed on to a beneficiary. If you intend to use a long-term (over 50 years) trust arrangement, you should see a lawyer.

If giving specific amounts, make certain that your estate will have sufficient funds. If not, the specific bequest will be reduced or eliminated. After all your specific bequests have been made, you can leave the remainder of your property to be divided among the beneficiaries or given to a charity or to whatever group of individuals you wish.

d. CAN YOU DISINHERIT A SPOUSE OR A CHILD?

Many people incorrectly believe that they can successfully disinherit a spouse or child by leaving him or her just one dollar. Provisions of the Wills Variation Act provide that a husband, wife, or child who was dependent on the deceased can apply to the courts to vary the terms of the will if he or she has been disinherited in this fashion. The courts will decrease the size of gifts to other beneficiaries to adequately provide for the applicant. The amount recoverable depends on the standard of living enjoyed by the applicant while living with the deceased, the size of the estate, and any special circumstances. Set out the reasons for the disinheritance in the will itself, for example:

> To my daughter Jane Doe, I leave $10, because during my lifetime I have already given her $20 000 which she has managed to squander. She has caused me much grief and unhappiness.

Since the disinherited party must apply to the courts to have the will varied, he or she may choose not to because of the resulting embarrassment. In addition, the power to vary the will is a discretionary power. If there appear to be strong reasons why the will should not be varied, the courts will probably not alter it. Each individual case has to be considered on its own merits.

If you seriously intend to disinherit a family member, you should ask your lawyer to draft a will incorporating the appropriate clause. If you attempt to do it yourself, you may be unsuccessful. Even with a lawyer, it is difficult to disinherit a spouse or a child. The Wills Variation Act enables a judge to decide what is just and equitable in the distribution of the deceased's assets. This is true even if his or her decision is entirely contrary to your wishes as expressed in your will.

To avoid this problem, you may have to provide an *inter vivos* trust (consult a lawyer to do this) or you may be able to avoid the problem by giving your assets away while you are alive. (The problem with the latter suggestion is that you may require these very assets to live on while you are alive.)

e. PAYMENT OF YOUR DEBTS

Your assets are distributed according to a set of priorities if there are insufficient funds to pay off your debts. Therefore, if you wish to make your specific gifts valid, assess your probable indebtedness and adjust your bequests accordingly. Do not forget to consider the debts that arise on your death, such as probate fees, legal fees, and funeral expenses.

If your estate has insufficient funds to cover all the debts after the specific bequests have been made, the money to pay debts is first taken out of the personal property in the residue of the estate (which is the remainder of the estate after all specific bequests have been allotted).

Personal property consists of all property except land and buildings and improvements upon the land. If this money is not enough, some will be taken out of pecuniary (money) gifts, then from specific bequests of personal property, and, last, if there are still insufficient funds to pay off debts, the real estate will be sold.

Remember, this encroachment on the gifts or legacies occurs only if there are insufficient funds to meet your debts after death.

If there is insufficient money in the estate to cover the debts alone, the priority of payment of the debts of the estate is as follows:

(a) Testamentary expenses (including funeral expenses and costs of probate)

(b) Income and gift taxes

(c) Liabilities as at the date of death

(d) In the case of probate, executor's fees, and in the case of administration, administrator's fees

f.   WHAT IS A HOLOGRAPH WILL?

A will signed only by the person making it and written entirely in his or her own handwriting is called a "holograph will." The advantage of a holograph will is that, as no witnesses are needed, someone can make a will when alone and near death. The disadvantages are that it is a little easier for an unscrupulous person to alter a will of this sort. If the dispositions are at all numerous or complicated, there is a great likelihood that confusion will arise concerning what the deceased actually meant (usually this type of will is drawn with no legal assistance whatever).

Alberta, Manitoba, and Saskatchewan all recognize this type of will as valid, but in British Columbia a will must be witnessed by two eligible people before it will be valid. So, even if you do a will entirely in your own handwriting, you must call in two witnesses before you sign it. An exception to this rule occurs when a person is in the armed forces on active duty or a sailor is in the course of a voyage; they may sign a will without witnesses and it will still be valid.

g. SUMMARY OF STEPS IN THE EXECUTION OF A WILL

If you are drafting your own will, remember the following:

(a) Make a draft of your will setting out the names of the people to whom you wish to give your property. Also list the specific amounts of gifts they are to receive. Be sure that all beneficiaries and the nature of the gift to them is clearly identified. Note that if you have left something to an adult child who predeceases you, that child's share will go to his or her children, if any, rather than to your other children.

(b) Name the executor and an alternative executor.

(c) Adapt precedents similar to those in the following samples to your particular requirements. Type or clearly handwrite the document but do not sign it. You may wish to take advantage of the blank will forms that are available from the publisher. Keep in mind that most of these forms lack "alternative executor" or beneficiary clauses such as the "30-day clause" discussed earlier, so be prepared to add such clauses.

(d) Call in two witnesses, who must be 19 years of age or older and who are not beneficiaries named in the will. The two witnesses must be present together and must actually see you and each other sign.

(e) First, with the witnesses watching, initial each page of the document and sign the final page. Then have both witnesses initial each page and sign in the appropriate places opposite your signature on the final page.

(f) Be certain the proper date is inserted in the document. The proper date is the day it is signed.

(g) Place your valid will in a safe, fireproof place and tell your executor where it is. Remember, if you make copies of your will, sign the original only. Never sign the copy, or it will become your last will since the law presumes that a copy is signed after the original is signed. By signing the copy of the will, you create a legal dilemma especially if the original cannot be found. The court will not know if you destroyed the original with an intention to revoke it or if you intended the copy to become your last will and testament.

h. FILING A WILLS NOTICE

After your will has been drawn according to your wishes and properly signed and witnessed, I recommend that you file a Wills Notice. You can do this by completing a simple form like the one shown in Sample #2.

The Wills Notice serves to record the existence and location of the will in, for example, your safety deposit box, your lawyer's safe, or your home. This helps prevent confusion if problems arise after your death. The notice is filed at the Vital Statistics Agency in Vancouver for a nominal fee ($17 at the time of writing), and acknowledgment of the notice is mailed to you from the department.

The notice form may be obtained free of charge by mail from the Vital Statistics Agency:

British Columbia Vital Statistics Agency
PO Box 9657 STN Prov Govt
Victoria, B.C.
V8W 9P3

or from your local Vital Statistics Agency office (details in Appendix 2). Keep the acknowledgment with the will or give it to your personal representative along with a copy of the will.

When you revise, revoke, or change the location of your will, you should complete section (b) or (c), whichever is applicable, of a new Wills Notice rather than section (a) as in our example. The Vital Statistics Agency files this notice too. When a search is requested after your death, a form setting out the particulars of all Wills Notices on file is returned to the executor or the lawyer.

The notice bearing the latest date is to confirm the existence of the last will and testament, unless a valid will bearing a later date is found after the death.

It is not legally mandatory that you file such a notice, but it is strongly recommended particularly when you have made more than one will during your lifetime. You should file one because the law requires your executor or administrator to have the department conduct a search as a preliminary requirement to obtaining Letters of Probate or Letters of Administration.

If you have filed notices of all wills and codicils that you have made, confusion will be eliminated, particularly if any previous will or its copy had not been destroyed.

How to search for a Wills Notice is discussed in section **d.** of chapter 3.

SAMPLE #2
WILLS NOTICE

BRITISH COLUMBIA
Ministry of Health and
Ministry Responsible for Seniors

WILLS NOTICE

BRITISH COLUMBIA
VITAL STATISTICS AGENCY
PO BOX 9657 STN PROV GOVT
Victoria BC V8W 9P3
Phone: (250) 952-2681

VITAL STATISTICS CLIENT NUMBER *(If known)*	SHADED AREA FOR OFFICE USE ONLY

MAILING ADDRESS: Name and address of Testator or firm submitting this notice. Please PRINT clearly.
Include POSTAL CODE.

Name Tammy Testator

Address 123 Wills Road

City, Prov./State, Country Vancouver, B.C.   *Postal Code* Z 1 P – 0 G 0

IF COMPANY,
ATTENTION:

WORK NUMBER 555-1234   FACSIMILE NUMBER 555-2345

Wills Notice dated this __1st__ day of __January__ , A.D. __200–__ *yyyy*

is filed respecting the will of __Tony Thomas__ __Testator__ __M__
(Given names in full)   (Surname)   (Sex)

IMPORTANT
We cannot register this notice without all these particulars

born on the __20th__ day of __August__ , A.D. __1930__ *yyyy*

at __Pouce Coupe__ __B.C.__ , occupation __Mechanic__
(City)   (Province or Country)

and now residing at __123 Wills Road__ __Vancouver__ __B.C.__ __ZIP 0G0__
(Number)   (Street)   (City or Place)   (Province or Country)   (Postal Code)

COMPLETE IN FULL! REMIT FEE OF $17.00

(a) HAVE (HAS) EXECUTED MY (HIS, HER) LAST WILL AND TESTAMENT AND/OR CODICIL bearing date the

__1st__ day of __January__ , A.D. __200–__ , which will and/or codicil is situated at *yyyy*

__Bank of Goldbrick__
(Name of place, trust company, bank, law office, etc.)

at __111 Low Street__ __Victoria__ __B.C.__ __Z1P 0G0__
(Street address)   (Name of city or place)   (Province)   (Postal Code)

(b) HAVE (HAS) REVOKED MY (HIS, HER) LAST WILL AND TESTAMENT AND/OR CODICIL bearing date the

_____ day of _____ , A.D. _____ , which will and/or codicil was situated at *yyyy*

_____
(Name of place, trust company, bank, law office, etc.)

at _____ _____ _____ _____
(Street address)   (Name of city or place)   (Province)   (Postal Code)

(c) HAVE (HAS) CHANGED THE LOCATION OF MY (HIS, HER) LAST WILL AND TESTAMENT AND/OR CODICIL

bearing date the _____ day of _____ , A.D. _____ , from *yyyy*

_____
(Name and address of place, trust company, bank, law office, etc. where will was formerly situated)

to _____
(Name and address of place, trust company, bank, law office, etc. where will is now situated)

TELEPHONE No. 555-6666   X *Tammy Testator*
(WRITTEN SIGNATURE OF TESTATOR OR SOLICITOR, NOTARY PUBLIC OR TRUST OFFICER ONLY)

HLTH 531 REV 99/08/09

i. HOW TO CHANGE ONE OR TWO CLAUSES IN THE WILL

Clauses in a will frequently have to be changed because, for example, a beneficiary dies or marries and has children. When you simply want to change one or two clauses in your will you can, instead of making a new will, add what is known as a "codicil". For example, say you wish to transfer a bequest to another person. Instead of changing the entire will, you can add a codicil in which you revoke the previous bequest and name a new beneficiary. A codicil is a "mini-will" and when properly completed has all the formality and validity of a complete will.

A codicil simply states:

> This is my codicil and is supplemental to my will dated the 12th day of July 1996. Paragraph 3 of my will is revoked and replaced by the following paragraph.
>
> Allan Doe shall receive my car rather than John Doe.

The codicil must be signed by you, the testator or testatrix, in the presence of two witnesses in the same manner as a will. (See Sample #7.) Make certain that you also date your codicil.

j. HOW OFTEN SHOULD YOU REVISE YOUR WILL OR MAKE A NEW ONE?

A valid will takes effect upon your death, no matter how long prior to death it was made. In the meantime, your financial position may have changed considerably for better or worse. Therefore, it is most important that you revise your will every few years. Good reasons for revision include a change in the tax laws (like the repeal of succession duties), a change in personal assets, the birth of a child or grandchild, the death of a named executor, or the death of one or more of the named beneficiaries. In many cases, the execution of a simple codicil (as already outlined) may be sufficient but, in others, a completely new will may have to be made.

For example, if you and your spouse separate, then you should both prepare new wills excluding your estranged spouse from your estate as soon as possible. You should seek the advice of a lawyer to ensure that your estranged spouse is not able to set aside your will. In addition, in the separation agreement you should include a clause such as the following:

> The wife releases and surrenders all claims which she has or might later have to share in any part of the estate of the husband if the husband predeceases the wife, except only to the extent that the husband may in his last will and testament otherwise provide; and, further, the wife waives and renounces any claim or right that she may later have to the administration or to share in the administration of the estate of the husband.

A similar clause would be included about the husband. Note that a divorce will also have a dramatic effect on your will (see page 3).

You make a new will in the same way as you made the first one. By making a new will you revoke the former one, which should be destroyed to avoid confusion. The most recent will is the one that becomes effective on your death.

k. CAN YOU REVOKE YOUR WILL?

A will is not a binding contract upon you once it is made. You can revoke or alter it at any time before death simply because you change your mind. You can make a will inoperative by the following means.

1. Destroy it

You can destroy your will by burning it, tearing it, or throwing it out in the garbage. Once destroyed, the will is treated as never having existed.

To validly revoke a will, you must destroy it with the intent that you no longer want the document to have effect as your last will and testament. An accidental tearing or burning is not sufficient, although it is up to the executors to prove that the acts done to the will were accidental, and this can be a problem in many cases. Although there have been cases in which the courts have held the validity of a will that is proven to have been accidentally destroyed, you shouldn't rely on these cases to protect you. If you have accidentally damaged your will, make a new one immediately so that there can be no costly confusion over whether or not you did or did not intend to revoke it.

You need not destroy copies of the will to effectively revoke it. Simply destroy the original will that is in your possession, although it is wise to contact anyone holding a copy of the will and ask him or her to send it to you so that you can destroy it also. Of course, you should make a new will as soon as possible.

It has been determined that if the person who made the will destroys it while insane, the will is not revoked. In this case, the courts have held that the person was incapable of forming the necessary intent to revoke.

2. Make a new will

You can state in a new will that you revoke all wills and codicils previously made by you. This is a standard clause in many wills, but legally you don't need to state this because, under the law, your most recent will is always the one that is given effect. This is the reason it is important to date all of your wills.

3. Marry

When you marry, any wills made prior to that marriage are automatically revoked. It is presumed that an earlier will could not in any way reflect your true intent regarding your spouse, as quite possibly you could have had no inkling of his or her existence when you drew up the will. Because your will is revoked by marriage, you would be wise to make a valid will at the earliest possible moment after marriage.

33

It would seem logically reasonable (but somewhat macabre) to recommend that a new will be prepared before the wedding day, but not signed and witnessed until immediately after the wedding ceremony prior to your departure for a reception or honeymoon. Unfortunately, tragic accidents do happen, and a will avoids the many potential problems that can arise from an accident on the honeymoon.

Probably the easiest, most sensible way to alleviate problems is to have your will carefully drawn by a lawyer in "contemplation of marriage" so it will be effective even after the wedding. Legal advice should be obtained to draw this type of will. (See Sample #8.)

Remember that revoking a will does not make an earlier will effective, as many unfortunate would-be beneficiaries have discovered. Once revoked the will is no longer valid. If only a copy of a revoked will is in existence at death, the assets of the estate are divided in accordance with the rules on intestacy (as if there were no will).

1. WHAT HAPPENS TO YOUR WILL WHEN YOU MOVE?

If you become a resident in another province or state, this may affect your will. If you were a resident of Alberta, which recognizes holograph wills (a will signed only by you and written completely in your handwriting), your will would be valid as long as you reside in Alberta. However, if you became a resident of British Columbia, the terms of the will could be ignored because that kind of will does not meet the requirements of wills of British Columbia residents (unless they are in the armed forces or are sailors in the course of a voyage).

Many provinces have community property laws that affect what assets you can bequeath under a will. It is best to make a new will as soon as possible after moving to a new province or state.

Also, tax laws differ among provinces, and a will with provisions that do not attract excessive tax in one province might do just the opposite in another. This same consideration applies if, for example, you take up residence in the United States or Mexico. For all of the above reasons it is best to have your will at least looked over whenever you move to a new province or state.

A final consideration is that if you have assets in "foreign" jurisdictions, your estate will have to pass through probate in all the provinces where assets like land, bank accounts, or shares are located. One way to save your executors the inconvenience and expense of making all of these applications is to form a small holding company in your new province to own all the assets. If you do this, then you can merely pass on the shares of the company to your beneficiaries and only one set of Letters Probate would be needed. However, you should still make a new will so that you may be certain that it complies with the will requirements of the new jurisdiction. Remember to consult an accountant or tax lawyer before incorporating a "holding company." An inactive holding company has a high income tax rate.

If you move to British Columbia from another area, be sure to file the Wills Notice in Vancouver so that there is official notice of the existence and location of the will. Better still, have the original will sent to you and place it safely in a nearby safety deposit box.

When you are drawing up your new will, try to appoint one local executor as it is very difficult for someone residing out of the province to look after all the details properly.

m. CAN YOUR WILL BE VOIDED?

Yes, your will can be voided, but there is a normal presumption that a person has testamentary capacity, that is, the ability to make a will. Once it has been established that the person had the necessary legal capacity to make a will and once the legal formalities have been complied with, it is presumed to be a valid will. Even a person who is a raving lunatic can have a valid will providing he or she gave the instructions during a lucid period and understood that the document dealt with the disposition of his or her personal property and real estate, etc., and the will was prepared in accordance with his or her instructions. In such a situation, it is strongly advised that a lawyer draw the will.

Assuming that the legal formalities have been followed and that the person had the necessary legal capacity to make a will, the burden of proof to set aside or challenge a will is on those attempting to set it aside. It is not sufficient reason to set aside a will because the person making it left assets to a person who is unrelated.

1.   Undue influence

No effect will be given to your directions if a beneficiary or relative can show that the terms in your will were the result of *undue influence* being exerted by a beneficiary or other interested person upon you. Undue influence in the legal context is an action that amounts to force and coercion and not merely the influence of affection or attachment. There must be proof that the act of making the will was obtained by this coercion — a forcefulness that could not be resisted. The beneficiary or some other person must have used physical or mental force and/or threatened some significant, unpleasant consequence that forced the person to make a will different from what he or she ordinarily would have done.

To be successful in challenging a will of this type, the beneficiaries must show, for example, that you were unduly influenced and coerced into making dispositions that you would not have ordinarily wanted to make. If it is proven that the will was made under these circumstances, the will is declared invalid and the estate passes as if no will had been drawn. It is, therefore, always recommended that if you are making an unusual bequest or giving assets to a non-relative, that you consult a lawyer.

2. Unsound mind

If a beneficiary or interested person can show that you were of unsound mind at the time you made the will, it will be voided in most situations, although a testator may have some minor delusions that would not affect the validity of the will. However, if it can be shown that you did not recognize the objects of your gifts (e.g., spouse or children) and your duty toward them because you felt that they were all dead or were about to murder you, then these beliefs would be sufficient to render the will invalid.

3. Formalities

If it can be shown that the statutory formalities were not complied with, then the will can be voided. The most common failures consist of improper witnessing (i.e., the beneficiaries witness the will or there are no witnesses) and improper signing of the will.

4. Marital status

The last situation that can make the terms of a will ineffective is a remarriage as was discussed earlier. The appointment of your spouse as executor and gifts to a spouse are void if you are divorced or separated by order of a court (see page 3).

As long as the will appears to be sensible and validly made, it is up to the people attacking it to prove on the balance of probabilities that the will was not properly made or does not properly reflect the wishes of the person making it.

SAMPLE #3
MASTER WILL

Preamble clause — Name and address of testator

> "THIS IS THE LAST WILL AND TESTAMENT of me, *Thomas Testator*, of the City of *Vancouver*, in the Province of *British Columbia*."

1. Revocation of earlier wills

> "I HEREBY REVOKE all wills and testamentary dispositions of every nature or kind whatsoever heretofore made by me."

2. Appointment of executors and trustees

> "I APPOINT *Ernie Executor* to be the executor and trustee of this, my will. I hereinafter refer to my executor and trustee as "Trustee.""

3. Provisions for substitute executors and trustees

> "But if my said trustee should refuse to act, predecease me, or die within a period of 30 days following my decease, then I appoint *Ernestine Executor* to be the executrix of my will."

4. Funeral wishes

> "I DIRECT MY remains to be cremated."

or

> "I DIRECT THAT I be buried in a simple manner and that all expenses in connection with my burial be kept to a bare minimum."

5. Appointment of guardian of infant children, effective on death of surviving spouse

> "IF MY *wife* predeceases me, then on my death I appoint *Bob Grante* to be the guardian of my infant children."

6. Realization clause — Payment of debts, funeral expenses, etc.

> "I DIRECT my trustee to pay my just debts, funeral, and testamentary expenses and all income taxes, estate, inheritance, and succession duties or taxes where-so-ever payable."

7. Bequest of personal articles

"To transfer and deliver absolutely my diamond ring to my daughter, *Shirley Testator*."

8. Cash legacies

"To pay the following cash legacies as soon after my death as practicable to such of the following named legatees as are alive at my death:

(a) $1 000 to my mother, *Emma Peal*;

(b) $500 to my friend, *Pamela Purdy*.

9. Bequest of everything to trustee to deal with according to specific instructions.

"I GIVE ALL of the residue of my property of every nature and kind and wherever situate to my trustee upon the following trusts:

(a) If my wife, *Clementine Testator*, survives me for 30 days, I direct my executor to pay or transfer to my wife the residue of my estate for her own use absolutely;

(b) If my wife predeceases me or, surviving me, dies within a period of 30 days following my decease, I direct my executor to divide the residue of my estate equally among my three children, *Shirley Testator*, *Terry Testator*, and *David Testator*, for their own use absolutely. Should any of my children predecease me, then the child or children of such deceased child, if any, shall be entitled to the share of their deceased parent, such share to be divided equally. If there are no children of such deceased child of mine, then the share of such deceased child shall be divided equally among those of my children who may be alive at my death.

10. Distribution of residue of estate

"I DIRECT my trustee to invest the residue of my estate as follows."

(a) Wide investment clause

"Unless provided otherwise, to invest and keep invested the residue of my estate and I declare that my executor when making investments for my estate shall not be limited to investments authorized by law, but may make any investments that in his uncontrolled discretion he considers advisable."

and

(b) Where infant children are involved

"To hold and keep invested the residue of my estate in trust, and the income and capital or as much as my trustee in his absolute discretion deems advisable be used for the benefit, maintenance, and education of my children then alive until the youngest reaches the age of 19 at which time my trustee shall divide the residue of my estate then remaining in equal shares among my children then alive."

(i) "Upon my demise, my trustee is to divide the residue of my estate into the number of shares equivalent in number to the number of children surviving me."

(ii) "As each child attains the age of nineteen, one such share shall be paid to each child for his or her own use absolutely."

(iii) "My trustee may encroach on such share providing it is for the benefit of the infant from whose share the funds are obtained."

(iv) "Any share not distributed due to the death of one of the beneficiaries shall be divided equally among my surviving children."

(c) If there are no children

"To pay or transfer the residue of my estate to my said wife if she survives me for 30 days for her own use absolutely."

IN WITNESS WHEREOF, I have hereunto set my hand this *20th* day of *June, 20__*.

SIGNED, PUBLISHED, AND DECLARED by the said testator, *Thomas Testator,* as and for his last will and testament, in the presence of us, both present at the same time, who at his request, and in his presence and in the presence of each other, have hereunto subscribed our names as witnesses.

Thomas Testator
(Testator signs here)

Q. C. Ewe
Witness

101 Probate Lane
Vancouver, B.C.
Address

Teacher
Occupation

U. R. Here
Witness

304 Testamentary Row
Vancouver, B.C.
Address

Legal Secretary
Occupation

SAMPLE #4
WILL FOR A MARRIED MAN
LEAVING ENTIRE ESTATE ABSOLUTELY TO
WIFE AND ADULT CHILDREN*

THIS IS THE LAST WILL AND TESTAMENT of me, *David Daniel Dede,* of the City of *Vancouver,* in the Province of *British Columbia.*

1. I REVOKE all former wills and other testamentary dispositions by me at any time heretofore made and declare this only to be and contain my last will and testament.

2. I APPOINT my wife to be the executrix of this my will. If she predeceases me, I appoint *Alan Eagleview* of the City of *Vancouver,* in the Province of *British Columbia,* to be the executor of this my will.

3. I DIRECT my executrix to pay out of the capital of my estate my just debts, funeral and testamentary expenses, and all income taxes, estate, inheritance, and succession duties or taxes wheresoever payable.

4. I GIVE the following legacies:

(a) If my wife survives me for 30 days, I GIVE, DEVISE, AND BEQUEATH the residue of my real and personal property whatsoever and wheresoever situate, including any property over which I may have a general power of appointment, to my wife.

(b) If, however, my wife predeceases me or fails to survive me for 30 days, then I GIVE all my real and personal property whatsoever and wheresoever situate, including any property over which I may have a general power of appointment, to my children, namely *Samuel, Bette,* and *Bobby* to be divided equally among them but only if they survive me for 30 days.

(c) If any of my children predecease me or fail to survive me for 30 days, then the child or children of such deceased child shall receive the share which the deceased child of mine would have been entitled to were he/she living at my death.

(d) Should any of my children predecease me or fail to survive me for 30 days without leaving children, then such share that such child would have received had he or she survived shall be transferred to my child or equally to my children who survive me for 30 days.

(e) Should my wife and my children fail to survive me for 30 days or fail to survive to receive their entire share of my estate, the residue of my estate is to be transferred to _____.

*The same form may be used by a married woman in favor of her husband and children.

IN WITNESS WHEREOF I have hereunto set my hand this *20th* day of *May,* *20__.*

SIGNED, PUBLISHED, AND DECLARED by the said testator, *David Daniel Dede,* as and for his last will and testament, in the presence of us, both present at the same time, who, at his request, in his presence and in the presence of each other, have hereunto subscribed our names as witnesses.

David Daniel Dede
(Testator signs here)

I. C. Ewe
Witness

321 Ocean Drive
Vancouver, B.C.
Address

Stenographer
Occupation

U. R. Here
Witness

1624 Westview Road
Vancouver, B.C.
Address

Cook
Occupation

SAMPLE #5
WILL WITH A TRUST ARRANGEMENT
FOR INFANT CHILDREN

THIS IS THE LAST WILL AND TESTAMENT of me, *Anne Toogood,* of the City of *Prince George,* in the Province of *British Columbia.*

1. I REVOKE all former wills and other testamentary dispositions of every nature or kind whatsoever made by me.

2. I APPOINT *Thor Toogood* of the City of *Prince George,* in the Province of *British Columbia,* to be the executor and trustee of this my will. Should the above-named individual predecease me or be unwilling or unable to act as my executor or trustee, then I HEREBY APPOINT *Edwin Executor* of the City of *Prince George,* in the Province of *British Columbia,* to be the executor and trustee (hereinafter referred to as my trustee of this my will).

3. I APPOINT *Thor Toogood* of the City of *Prince George,* in the Province of *British Columbia,* to be the guardian of the persons and estates of my infant children during their minority. If he predeceases me or is unwilling or unable to act, then I APPOINT *Thelma Toogood* to be the guardian of the persons and estates of my infant children during their minority.

4. I GIVE all my real and personal property whatsoever and wheresoever including any property over which I may have a general power of appointment to my said trustee upon the following trusts, namely:

(a) To use his discretion in the realization of my estate, with power to sell, call in, and convert into money any part of my estate not consisting of money at such time or times, in such manner and upon such terms, and either for cash or credit or for part cash and part credit as he may in his uncontrolled discretion decide upon, or to postpone such conversion of my estate or any part or parts for such length of time as he may think best, and I hereby declare that my executor may retain any portion of my estate in the form in which it may be at my death (notwithstanding that it may not be in the form of an investment in which trustees are authorized to invest trust funds and whether or not there is a liability attached to any such portion of my estate) for a length of time as he may in his discretion deem advisable, and he shall not be held responsible for any loss that may happen to my estate by reason of so doing;

(b) To pay out of the capital of my estate my just debts, funeral and testamentary expenses, and all outstanding taxes;

(c) To hold the residue of my estate in trust for my children alive at my death in equal shares. The share of each child shall be held and kept invested by my trustee. The income and capital, or as much as my trustee in his discretion considers advisable, shall be paid to or applied for the benefit of such child until he or she attains the age of majority. Four years after graduation from a post-secondary institution, the trustee shall transfer

SAMPLE #5 — Continued

to each child the capital and any income accruing, if not previously advanced. Should a child of mine die before attaining the age of majority, his or her share or the amount remaining, shall be held by my trustee in trust for the children (equally) of such deceased child, who survive him or her. Should any deceased child not have any child or children surviving him, then his or her share shall be equally divided among my other children.

(d) Any payments to be made to any infant beneficiary shall be deemed sufficiently made if paid to his or her guardian.

(e) Should my husband and my children fail to survive me for 30 days or fail to survive to receive their entire share of my estate, the undistributed residue of my estate is to be transferred to _____.

IN WITNESS WHEREOF I have hereunto set my hand this *2nd* day of *May,* 20__.

SIGNED, PUBLISHED, and DECLARED by the said testatrix, *Anne Toogood,* as and for her last will and testament, in the presence of us, both present at the same time, who, at her request, in her presence and in the presence of each other, have hereunto subscribed our names as witnesses.

_____
(Testatrix signs here)

I. C. Cwe
_____
Witness

131 Witnesses Road
Prince George, B.C.
_____
Address

Optometrist
_____
Occupation

U.L. Hele
_____
Witness

135 Witnesses Road
Prince George, B.C.
_____
Address

Health Inspector
_____
Occupation

45

SAMPLE #6
WILL DRAWN BY A SINGLE PERSON
IN FAVOR OF PARENTS FOR LIFE AND THEN
EQUALLY TO BROTHERS AND SISTERS ABSOLUTELY

THIS IS THE LAST WILL AND TESTAMENT of me, *Sarah Single*, of the City of *Victoria*, in the Province of *British Columbia*.

1. I REVOKE all former testamentary dispositions made by me and declare this to be my last will.

2. I APPOINT *Paul Prince*, of the City of *Victoria*, in the Province of *British Columbia*, to be the executor and trustee of this my will (hereinafter referred to as trustee). If the above-named individual predeceases me or is unwilling or unable to act as my executor and trustee, then I APPOINT *Paula Prince* to be the executrix and trustee of my will.

3. I GIVE all my real and personal property whatsoever and wheresoever situate including any property over which I may have a general power of appointment to my said trustee upon the following trusts, namely:

(a) To use his discretion in the realization of my estate, with power to my trustee to sell, call in, and convert into money any part of my estate not consisting of money at such time or times, in such manner and on such terms, and either for cash or credit or for part cash and part credit as he may in his uncontrolled discretion decide on, or to postpone such conversion of my estate or any part or parts thereof for such length of time as he may think best, and I declare that my trustee may retain any portion of my estate in the form in which it may be at my death (notwithstanding that it may not be in the form of an investment in which trustees are authorized to invest trust funds and whether or not there is a liability attached to any such portion of my estate) for such length of time as he may in his discretion deem advisable, and he shall not be held responsible for any loss that may happen to my estate by reason of so doing;

(b) To pay out of the capital of my estate my just debts, funeral and testamentary expenses, and all outstanding taxes;

(c) To hold the residue of my estate in trust for my mother and father alive at my death in equal shares provided that the share of each parent of mine who shall be living at my death shall be held and kept invested by my trustee and the income and capital or so much thereof as my trustee in his discretion considers advisable shall be paid to or applied for the benefit of my mother and father and survivor of them.

4. After the death of the survivor of my father and mother to pay the residue of my estate to my brothers and sisters, then living, equally.

SAMPLE #6 — Continued

IN WITNESS WHEREOF I have hereunto set my hand this *12th day* of *June,* *20__.*

SIGNED, PUBLISHED, and DECLARED by the said testatrix, *Sarah Single,* as and for her last will and testament, in the presence of us, both present at the same time, who, at her request, in her presence and in the presence of each other, have hereunto subscribed our names as witnesses.

Sarah Single
(Testatrix signs Here)

A.M. Witness
Witness

305 Long Road
Victoria, B.C.
Address

Sales Manager
Occupation

I.C. Ewe.
Witness

605 Narrow Bend
Victoria, B.C.
Address

Engineer
Occupation

SAMPLE #7
CODICIL

THIS IS THE FIRST CODICIL to the last will of me, *Tom Toogood*, which last will bears the date of the *16th* day of *January, 20___*.

1. I DIRECT that the first paragraph of clause three be deleted and the following clause be substituted therefor:

If my wife, *Tess Toogood*, predeceases me or survives me but dies within 30 days following my decease, I APPOINT my daughter, *Bess Toogood*, to be the executrix and trustee of this my will.

2. I REVOKE clause five (a) of my last will.

3. In all other respects, I confirm my last will.

IN WITNESS WHEREOF, I, *Tom Toogood*, have to this first codicil to my last will contained on this single sheet of paper subscribed my name at the City of *Kelowna*, in the Province of *British Columbia*, on this *25th* day of *April, 20___*.

SIGNED, PUBLISHED, and DECLARED by *Tom Toogood*, the above-named testator, as and for this first codicil to his last will, in the presence of us, who in his presence at his request and in the presence of each other, have hereunto subscribed our names as witnesses, attesting the same.

_____
(Testator signs here)

_____
Witness

2120 Right Way
Kelowna, B.C.
Address

Professor
Occupation

_____
Witness

331 River Way
Kelowna, B.C.
Address

Retailer
Occupation

SAMPLE #8
PORTION OF A WILL MADE
IN CONTEMPLATION OF MARRIAGE

THIS IS THE LAST WILL AND TESTAMENT of me, *Tom Jones,* of the City of *Vancouver,* in the Province of *British Columbia,* made in contemplation of my marriage to *Susan Sweet.*

1. I HEREBY REVOKE all wills and testamentary dispositions of every nature or kind whatsoever made by me.

2. IF MY MARRIAGE to *Susan Sweet* is solemnized, I nominate, constitute and appoint *Susan Sweet* to be sole executrix and trustee of this my will. But if she should predecease me or die within 30 days following my decease, then on the death of the survivor of me and *Susan Sweet,* or, if my marriage to *Susan Sweet* is not solemnized, I appoint *Ernest Edwin* (hereinafter referred to as my trustee) to be the executor and trustee of this my will in the place of the said *Susan Sweet.*

(This will then proceeds to give the trustee instructions as to distribution.)

3

EXECUTORS AND PROBATE

a. WHAT IS AN EXECUTOR AND HOW DO YOU CHOOSE ONE?

An *executor* is a man appointed in a will who is authorized to obtain legal title to the assets of the deceased so that he can gather them up and pay all the debts of the estate. An *executrix* is a woman who is appointed in the will to carry out these same functions. Both an executrix and an executor may be called the "personal representative" of the deceased person. After probate, which confirms the appointment of the executor named in the will, he or she distributes the balance of the assets to the beneficiaries in accordance with the terms in the will. He or she does this after deducting administrative, funeral, and taxation expenses (if any). Ensure that your executor or executrix is a Canadian resident to avoid income tax problems due to the estate being classified as a "non-resident estate."

You should select an executor or executrix who is reliable and trustworthy, and should be young enough to outlive you. If you do not appoint a personal representative in your will, or if your personal representative dies before you do and you neglect to change your will, your next-of-kin (usually spouse or eldest adult child) must apply to be appointed as an *administrator* or *administratrix*. The duties of the administrator (or administratrix) are the same as the executor (or executrix); it is the appointment that is different. Because the courts are in charge of appointing an administrator (or administratrix), delays in settling the estate can occur. Therefore, you should always appoint an alternative personal representative when you make your will so that he or she can take over where the first one left off.

Your personal representative must be capable of fully exercising his or her legal rights. You may not appoint as your executor someone who has been legally declared insane. Apart from this restriction, you may name almost any person over the age of 19 who, for practical reasons, should be a British Columbia resident at the time you are making your will. If you appoint your spouse as executor and later divorce, that appointment will be revoked under the Wills Act (see page 3).

The person you appoint in your will derives his or her powers directly from the will and the formal procedure of probate merely confirms the appointment. The Grant of Letters Probate is evidence of this confirmation that can be shown to debtors and creditors of the estate.

b. THE POWERS OF A PERSONAL REPRESENTATIVE

How does a person who has been appointed an executor or executrix in a deceased person's will indicate his or her acceptance of the appointment? Acts such as locking up the residence of the deceased and preparing an inventory of the deceased's assets are not considered by the courts to be acts of executorship. But such acts as entering into a contract to sell goods or assets of the estate are acts of executorship.

A person who intermeddles in the estate is called an "executor de son tort" (executor by his or her own wrongful act) and is liable to the co-executors. An intermeddler can also be sued by the deceased's creditors and heirs and held responsible for making up the difference between the amount that a reasonable person would have obtained for the estate and the amount actually obtained by the executor de son tort.

A personal representative may make expenditures on your behalf such as funeral and other reasonable expenses.

51

Your station in life is taken into consideration in determining whether or not funeral expenses are reasonable and, if expenditures are proved to be unreasonable, your executor is personally liable for the difference between a reasonable amount and the price actually paid.

Your executor or executrix is able to do anything that you would be able to do. For example, the executor normally has the power to take possession of the deceased's effects, pay debts owed by the deceased, accept monies owed to the deceased, collect rent due to the deceased, and sell, or otherwise dispose of, the goods and property of the deceased.

An executrix or executor must notify the beneficiaries of the death and tell them of their entitlement under the will. You often see a notice to creditors and others who might have a claim against the estate published in the newspapers. (See Sample #9.) This is required under the provisions of the Trustee Act, but may be dispensed with if all debts are known and all beneficiaries agree to waive its publication.

SAMPLE #9
NOTICE TO CREDITORS

IN THE MATTER OF THE ESTATE OF

John James Jesse
formerly of Suite 201 - 1170 Any Street
Anytown, British Columbia

NOTICE IS HEREBY GIVEN that creditors and others having claims against the estate of John James Jesse, deceased, are required to send full particulars of such claims to the undersigned solicitors for the estate, on or before the 30th day of June, 20__, after which date the executrix will distribute the estate's assets having regard only to the claims of which she has notice.

Mary Jane Jesse
Executrix

Smith, Smith, Smith, and Smith
Barristers and Solicitors,
5678 Capricorn Street
Anytown, British Columbia

Creditors have a right to recover from the beneficiaries at any time, if they can prove their claims against the estate. The advertisements serve to protect the personal representative only from personal liability for debts. It is usually sufficient for the personal representative to carefully look into the deceased's affairs to find existing creditors, complete a standard form notice and mail copies to the immediate family and any beneficiaries named in the will.

If it is necessary, the executor can bring legal action before receiving the Grant of Letters Probate, but the lawsuit may not be maintained until probate is confirmed.

In summary, then, an executor or executrix becomes the legal owner of all assets of the deceased and must distribute them according to the provisions in the will. Executors and executrices can pass on or assign their offices. A testator may give his personal representative the power to appoint a new executor by including in the will a clause such as the following:

> I hereby grant to my executor the right to nominate
> or appoint an alternative executor to replace him.

Even without this clause, your executor would pass on his powers of appointment in his own will if he were to die. Thus, the executor named in your executor's will would become responsible for both estates (yours and your executor's). If the executor left no will, an intestacy would result. His administrator would not become responsible for your estate because an administrator is not someone in whom the executor had special confidence. Another administrator, usually one of your close next-of-kin, would have to be appointed to look after your estate.

c. IMMEDIATE PROVISION FOR SURVIVORS

Executors and executrices have the power to take possession of items in a safety deposit box 14 days after the bank has mailed a list of the box's contents to the Minister of Finance.

As mentioned previously, when a person dies, his or her assets are "frozen." Generally, they may not be dealt with until the will is probated (or until the administrator is appointed, as the case may be) and the necessary probate releases (if applicable) obtained.

The following are exceptions to this rule. In other words, these assets may be dealt with without the consent of the Minister of Finance.

(a) If the deceased has an insurance policy payable to a named beneficiary other than an executor, the insurance company may pay the entire amount to that beneficiary. In the case of insurance proceeds, the insurance company would *usually* require the following documents before paying out the amounts indicated above.

   (i) Original of the insurance policy (if available)

   (ii) The death certificate

   (iii) A claimant's statement provided by the insurance company to be filled in by the claimant (i.e., the beneficiary)

   (iv) The attending physician's statement or report form, usually provided by the insurance company, to be filled in by the physician declaring the death

(b) When money is payable from a pension fund or plan of the deceased to a named beneficiary, this may be paid. The company should always be called in advance for the exact requirements. In the case of a pension fund or plan, the following documents are usually required before the money will be paid.

   (i) A beneficiary's claim statement provided by the trustees of the pension plan

   (ii) A death certificate

   (iii) Proof of identity of the claimant

(c) When the deceased was residing in the province, any branch of any bank, trust company, mortgage corporation, insurance company, other corporation, savings and loan association, or credit union shall transfer all money held in a joint account in the name of the deceased to the surviving joint tenant. In this case, the institution or person holding funds to the credit of the deceased would usually require the following documents before paying the money out.

    (i) A death certificate

    (ii) Proof of identity of the surviving joint tenant

If you hold a bank account jointly with the deceased, this money passes to you by operation of the right of survivorship. All you require is a death certificate. This also applies to all assets held in joint tenancy.

In all of the above matters, the party paying out the money must notify the Minister of Finance immediately, in writing in a notice form, stating that this money is being paid and the relationship of the party to whom the money is being paid.

d. HOW TO SEARCH FOR A WILLS NOTICE

Before a personal representative can receive Letters Probate, he or she must conduct a Search of Wills Notices through the Vital Statistics Agency and receive the completed notice indicating the results of the search. If a lawyer handles the estate, he or she simply fills out the form and sends it to the Vital Statistics Agency.

If you are doing it yourself, you must include a copy of the death certificate with the Application for Search of Wills Notice (Sample #11) and applicable fee. The charge for a wills search is $20 for the first name searched, and $5 for each additional name. Tony Thomas Testator, a.k.a. Tony Frederick Testator, a.k.a. Tony Thomas Smith, would be considered three names and three searches, requiring a fee of $30.

In most cases, it is easiest to obtain the death certificate by completing the form shown in Sample #10. This form, the Application for Marriage or Death Certificate, can be obtained from your nearest Vital Statistics office (see Appendix 2).

Be sure to give all the names that the deceased used to register property, stocks, bonds, or vehicles. You cannot get Letters Probate granted for all versions of the name if you have not conducted a wills search. If you have all versions of the deceased's name you can easily transfer property or stock without obtaining extra affidavits, which state for example, that A.S. Smith is the same as Alberta Susan Smith.

e. WHAT IS PROBATE?

Probate is a procedure by which the will of a deceased person is legally approved, confirmed, and documented. It also confirms the appointment of the executor.

Many people who have been appointed in a will have asked, "Can I do my own probating?" The answer is yes, provided there are no complex real estate transfers and no major tax considerations. These areas are very complex and you would be wise to see a lawyer, though executors and executrices can perform many of the duties described below even in the most complicated areas. As a general rule, a lawyer will charge about 2% of the gross (not net) value of the estate. This can quickly reach a substantial figure. (See section j. of this chapter for more information.) The rate charged is negotiable for simple estates.

This book contains a general outline of probate and administration procedures for your interest only. If you intend to actually probate an estate, it is recommended that you purchase the *Probate Guide for British Columbia*, another title in the Self-Counsel Series. It contains complete step-by-step instructions for probating an estate. The information on probate in this chapter is in no way to be considered a substitute

SAMPLE #10
APPLICATION FOR MARRIAGE OR DEATH
(Certificate or Registration Photocopy)

BRITISH COLUMBIA

Ministry of Health and
Ministry Responsible for Seniors
BRITISH COLUMBIA
VITAL STATISTICS AGENCY

APPLICATION FOR MARRIAGE OR DEATH
CERTIFICATE OR REGISTRATION PHOTOCOPY

MAILING ADDRESS INFORMATION	SHADED AREAS FOR OFFICE USE ONLY

NOTE: Please PRINT your name, address and identifying information clearly. This portion will be used when mailing your service or correspondence.

SURNAME	GIVEN NAMES
Testator	Tammy

MAILING ADDRESS
123 Wills Road

CITY, PROVINCE /STATE, COUNTRY	POSTAL CODE
Vancouver, B.C.	Z 1 P 0 G 0

HOME NUMBER	WORK NUMBER	FACSIMILE NUMBER
	555-1234	555-2345

APPLICANT'S CLIENT NUMBER
(FOR CORPORATE OR GOVERNMENT CLIENTS)

MARRIAGE — Groom's Details / Bride's Details

DATE & PLACE OF MARRIAGE	Month (abbreviated)	Day	Year	City	Province BRITISH COLUMBIA
GROOM'S SURNAME					
GIVEN NAMES	First		Middle Names		
BIRTH PLACE	City		Province/State		Country
BRIDE'S SURNAME *					*NOTE: SURNAME BEFORE MARRIAGE
GIVEN NAMES	First		Middle Names		
BIRTH PLACE	City		Province/State		Country

NOTE: ONLY LARGE SIZE DEATH CERTIFICATES ARE AVAILABLE

DEATH — Death Details

SURNAME	Testator						
GIVEN NAMES & SEX	First Tony Thomas			Middle Names		AGE 75	☒ MALE ☐ FEMALE
DATE & PLACE OF DEATH	Month (abbreviated) A U G	Day 2 1	Year 2 0 0 –	City Vancouver		Province BRITISH COLUMBIA	
PERMANENT RESIDENCE BEFORE DEATH	City Vancouver	Province/State B.C.	Country Canada	Place of Birth (City, Province/State, Country) Pouce Coupe, B.C.			

NUMBER OF SERVICES REQUIRED (see reverse for fee information)

☐ Certificate (Small) } regular service - $27.00 per certificate
☐ Certificate (Large) } (average 10 day processing time)

☐ Marriage Registration Photocopy, regular service - $50.00 per photocopy
☐ Marriage Registration Photocopy, rush 24 hour service - $60.00 per photocopy

☐ Certificate (Small) } rush 24 hour service - $60.00 per certificate
☐ Certificate (Large) }

NOTE: All services, other than rush services, will be mailed. Rush services are generated within 24 hours of receipt of request, and courier returned.

PAYMENT METHOD   SUBMITTED BY

☐ Cheque .... ☐ Mail ☐ In Person
☐ Money Order .... ☐ Mail ☐ In Person
☐ Credit Card (complete Credit Card section on the right)
Interac/Cash payment may be made in person at one of our four offices

AMOUNT ENCLOSED $_____

CREDIT CARD   SUBMITTED BY

☐ Visa .... ☐ Mail
☐ MasterCard .... } ☐ Phone
☐ American Express .... } ☐ Fax

Credit Card number: # _____
Card holder name as shown on Credit Card _____
Expiry date _____
Card holder signature _____

NOTE: The additional cost for credit card transactions ($5.95) is collected by Vital Chek for shipping and handling fees.

YOUR RELATIONSHIP TO EVENT ☐ Self ☐ Mother ☐ Father ☒ Spouse ☐ Other:_____

REASON CERTIFICATE REQUIRED: To apply for Letters Probate

YOUR SIGNATURE (written): *Tammy Testator*

HLTH 430m Rev.96/07/09

PLEASE READ NOTES ON REVERSE OF THIS FORM

SAMPLE #11
APPLICATION FOR SEARCH OF WILLS NOTICE

BRITISH COLUMBIA	Ministry of Health and Ministry Responsible for Seniors VITAL STATISTICS AGENCY	APPLICATION FOR SEARCH OF WILLS NOTICE

APPLICANT'S INFORMATION	SHADED AREAS FOR OFFICE USE ONLY

APPLICANT'S PERSONAL HEALTH NUMBER

APPLICANT'S DATE OF BIRTH
MONTH   DAY   YEAR

APPLICATION FOR SERVICE NUMBER

SURNAME: Testator   GIVEN NAMES: Tammy

APPLICANT'S MAILING ADDRESS: 123 Wills Road

CITY, PROV./STATE, COUNTRY: Vancouver, B.C.   POSTAL CODE: Z1P 0G0

APPLICANT'S CLIENT NUMBER

IF COMPANY:

ATTENTION:

HOME NUMBER: WORK NUMBER: 555-1234   FACSIMILE NUMBER: 555-2345

(FOR CORPORATE OR GOVERNMENT CLIENTS)

Complete either Section A or Section B, then complete Section C

SECTION A APPLICATION FOR WILLS SEARCH	SECTION B SOLICITORS OR NOTARIES ONLY

A certificate of death, statutory declaration or like document proving to the satisfaction of the Director of Vital Statistics that the person named as Testator had died and the search fee must accompany this application when requesting a search.

I, _____ am;
☐ (a) a solicitor of the Supreme Court of British Columbia
☐ (b) a member of the society of Notaries Public of British Columbia
1) acting on behalf of the below listed individual I request a Living Will Search ☐ or,
2) after due investigation, I believe the below named individual, died on _____
at _____

Tammy Testator
Written signature of applicant

Written signature of solicitor/notary

SECTION C SEARCH REQUEST DETAILS OF DECEASED PERSON	

Date of birth Aug. 20, 1930   Place of birth Pouce Coupe, B.C.

Full name (Surname, Given Names) Tony Thomas Testator

Also known as (Surname, Given Names) _____

Also known as (Surname, Given Names) _____

Also known as (Surname, Given Names) _____

For Same Day (24 hour rush) Service Requested and Provided _____

FEE
$20.00
+ $5.00
+ $5.00
+ $5.00
+ $33.00
TOTAL: _____

SPACE BELOW FOR VITAL STATISTICS AND COURT USE ONLY

FOR COURT REGISTRY USE ONLY
WILLS NOTICE No. : _____
PLACE OF ISSUANCE: _____
DATE OF ISSUANCE: _____
DATE OF WILL: _____
COURT REGISTRY No. : _____

HLTH 532 REV 99/05/31   PLEASE READ NOTES ON REVERSE OF THIS FORM

58

for the *Probate Guide for British Columbia*. **Do not** attempt to probate an estate using only information in this book.

You should keep in mind that it is not possible to deal with all of the problems that can arise when making a will or processing an estate. Legal advice is essential in difficult or unusual situations, although this book together with the *Probate Guide* should make it easier for most people to handle ordinary estates themselves.

As mentioned, probate requires a search at the Vital Statistics Agency records to ensure that there is no later-dated will than the one about to be probated. The following documents must then be filed in the probate division of the nearest Supreme Court Registry of British Columbia. All of these forms are shown at the end of this section.

1. Affidavit of Executor

This document is sworn by the executor(s) and must have the original will attached as an exhibit. This affidavit (or oath) states that the one or more applicants are the personal representatives named in the will. Other personal representatives who are named in the will but are not applying must be accounted for. They must have either died, renounced, or be reserving their right to apply. The last case usually occurs when an executor is far away or does not wish to be bothered. (See Sample #12.)

2. Notice form

This notice is sent to all beneficiaries and persons under the Wills Variation Act (spouse and children). (See Sample #13.)

3. Section 135(6) Affidavit of Executor

This is a document in which the personal representative swears that the notices above have been sent to the various beneficiaries indicating that he or she, the person signing the notice, is applying for Letters Probate or Administration. (See Sample #14.)

4. Disclosure statement

This is a document required by the probate department in Victoria, but it is filed with the probate registry closest to you. The statement lists the land and other assets and debts of the deceased. (See Sample #15.)

Part IV of the statement lists all the named beneficiaries and the value of property passing to them. It sets out the full names and other information pertaining to all beneficiaries, and their relationship to the deceased.

When completing the statement, be sure to list the correct legal description of the property as it would appear on a Freehold Transfer Form (previously called Transfer of an Estate in Fee Simple). You will not be able to transfer the property if the release refers to a different lot than the one actually owned by the deceased.

Recently, the government has suggested that more information be provided than was previously required. When dealing with real estate, they ask for the street address (civic address), whether the deceased's interest is a fee simple, mortgage interest, or is subject to an agreement for sale. The B.C. Assessment Authority "total actual value" is to be provided in addition to the market value. Strangely enough, the guidelines refer to disclosing any interest that the deceased had in joint tenancy. The reasoning for this is unclear, since you do not pay probate filing fees on the interest held in joint tenancy.

If the assets are partly comprised of shares, then the actual name in which the securities are registered is to be provided. Also, if the deceased owned an automobile or motor vehicle, then both the licence number as well as the serial number should be provided.

5. Search of Wills Notice

An Application for Search of Wills Notice is available at the Vital Statistics Agency and has already been discussed (see section **d.** and Sample #11).

6. Praecipe

When the above forms are submitted to the probate registry, they have attached to them a "Praecipe" which, for the purposes of probate, is a short covering document that sets out what it is that you are seeking (i.e., a Grant of Letters Probate) and merely serves as an instructional letter directed to the court clerks. (See Sample #16.)

When you complete the Praecipe, you can insert along with your request for a Grant of Letters Probate a request for the number of certified court copies that you will need to transfer assets like property and the number of office copies of the disclosure statement that will be needed to file with the land title office to transfer property from the deceased's name to yours as the personal representative. The probate clerks will tell you the fees to submit for these copies.

f. PROBATE FILING FEES

The personal representative must pay a filing fee based on the gross value of all the real and personal property of the deceased situated in the province that passes to the personal representative. In some cases, this could cause inequities because the debts or liabilities of the deceased are not taken into account. This could result in an insolvent estate being required to pay a filing fee even though there is insufficient money in the estate.

Estates under $10 000 are exempt from filing fees. The filing fee on the amounts between $10 000 and $25 000 is $200 and the excess over $25 000 is assessed at $6 for every thousand or part of a thousand over and above the $25 000. Estates over $50 000 have a filing fee of $358 plus $14 per $1 000 for

No. __12345__

Registry __Vancouver__

IN THE SUPREME COURT OF BRITISH COLUMBIA

Re: The Estate of __Tony Thomas Testator__ , Deceased

Affidavit of Executor

I __Tammy Thomasina Testator, of 123 Wills Road, Vancouver, Clerk__
Name, address, and occupation

MAKE OATH AND SAY THAT:

(1) Name in full

1. (1) __Tony Thomas Testator__

(2) Street address and city

late of (2) __123 Wills Road, Vancouver__

in the Province of __British Columbia__

(3) Occupation

(3) __Retired__ , died on the __21st__ day of __August__ ,

20 __0-__ at __Vancouver__ in the __Province__ of __British Columbia__ .

(4) Add codicils, if any

2. I believe Exhibit "A" to this affidavit to be the deceased's original last will which is dated the

__1st__ day of __January__ , 20 __0-__ .(4) _____

3. I am __sole__ executor(s) named in the will. (My appointment has not been revoked under Section 16 of the Wills Act by reason of a decree of judicial separation, divorce, or nullity granted after the date of the will in respect of a marriage of the deceased.) [*If any executors named in the will are not applying, explain why.*]

4. To the best of my knowledge, the deceased did/did not marry or remarry after the date of the will.

5. To the best of my knowledge the will is/is not witnessed by a person to whom, or to whose then wife or husband, a beneficial devise, bequest or other disposition or appointment is given or made.

6. I have made a diligent search and inquiry to ascertain the assets and liabilities of the deceased.

SELF-COUNSEL PRESS – PROBATE-BC (2-1)00

SAMPLE #12 — Continued

7. The statement marked exhibit "B" to this affidavit discloses the assets and liabilities of the deceased, irrespective of their nature, location or value, which pass to the deceased's personal representative, together with the names and addresses of the beneficiaries, their relationship to the deceased and the property passing to them.

8. I will disclose forthwith to the Court the existence of any asset or liability which has not been disclosed in Exhibit "B" hereto when I learn of the same.

9. I will administer according to law all of the estate which by law devolves to and vests in the personal representative of the deceased and I will exhibit a true and perfect inventory of the estate and render a just and true account thereof whenever required by law to do so.

SWORN before me at the _City_

of _Vancouver_ _____ in the Province

of _B.C._ ____ this _15th_ ____ day   *Tammy Testator*

of _September_ ____, 20 _0-_.

_____ *l. M. Commissioner* _____
A Commissioner, etc.

SELF-COUNSEL PRESS – PROBATE-BC (2-2)00

No. 12345

Registry Vancouver

IN THE SUPREME COURT OF BRITISH COLUMBIA

Re: The Estate of Tony Thomas Testator _____, Deceased

Notice of Intent to
Apply for Probate

IN THE ESTATE OF Tony Thomas Testator _____

of the City _____ of Vancouver _____, in the Province of British Columbia,

(Occupation) Retired _____, who died on the 21st _____ day of August _____,

20 0- _____

TAKE NOTICE that the undersigned is applying for Probate of the above estate in the Supreme Court of British

Columbia at Vancouver _____, British Columbia.

Tammy Testator
_____
(Signature)

Tammy Testator
_____
(Applicant)

ADDRESS OF REGISTRAR

800 Smithe Street
Vancouver, B.C.

123 Wills Road, Vancouver, B.C.
_____
(Address)

SELF-COUNSEL PRESS – PROBATE-BC (4-1)XX

No.__12345_____

Registry__Vancouver_____

IN THE SUPREME COURT OF BRITISH COLUMBIA

Re: The Estate of__Tony Thomas Testator_____, Deceased

Affidavit of Notice

I__Tammy Thomasina Testator_____
_____*Name, address, and occupation*

of the__City_____ of__Vancouver_____, in the province of British Columbia,

MAKE OATH AND SAY:

1. THAT I am the applicant for the Probate of the last Will and Testament bearing the date of__the 1st__ day of__January_____, 20_0-_, of__Tony Thomas Testator_____, deceased.

2. THAT I have mailed a notice in the form prescribed by Section 112(6) of the Estate Administration Act, along with a copy of the Will, by regular mail, postage prepaid, to each of the following who are, to the best of my knowledge, beneficiaries; a true copy of the Notice being marked Exhibit "A" to this my affidavit.

Name	Address	Relationship
Thomas Anthony Testator	456 Legacy Way, Prince George, BC	Son
Thelma Ann Brown	789 Rich Way, Nakusp, BC	Daughter
St. Elmo's Church	321 Shipyard Road, Victoria, BC	

3. THAT I have also mailed a Notice in the form prescribed by Section 112(6) of the said Act along with a copy of the Will to the following persons who are the only persons entitled to apply under the Wills Variation Act, with respect to the said Will or who would be entitled under an intestacy or partial intestacy, or who is a spouse who has been separated from the deceased for a period of more than one year.

Name	Address	Relationship
Thomas Anthony Testator	456 Legacy Way, Prince George, BC	Son
Thelma Ann Brown	789 Rich Way, Nakusp, BC	Daughter

4. THAT no person is a common-law spouse of the deceased as defined by Section 1 of the Estate Administration Act.

5. THAT to the best of my knowledge there are no other persons entitled to share in the said estate or entitled under an intestacy or partial intestacy.

SWORN BEFORE ME at the__City_____ of

__Vancouver_____ in the Province of

__BC_____, this_15th_____ day of

__October__, 20_0-_.   *Tammy Testator*

L . M . Commissioner

A Commissioner etc.

NOTE: *Please check Estate Administration Act, Section 112(3) for obtaining Order when person entitled has since died or whereabouts unknown, and Section 112(4) and (5) for mailing of notice to minors or mentally disordered persons.*

SELF-COUNSEL PRESS – PROBATE-BC (3-1)00

SAMPLE #15
DISCLOSURE STATEMENT

Estate of _Tony Thomas Testator_ _____, Deceased

Assets, Liabilities and Distribution

PART I	Real Property (Including mortgages and vendors and purchasers interests in agreements for sale)	Within or Without B.C.	Value at Death
Residence at 123 Wills Road, Vancouver, BC Legal description: Lot 6, Block 40, D.L. 526 Registered owners: Tony Thomas Testator Appraised Value: $120,711.87		Within BC	
	TOTAL		$120,711.87

PART II	Personal Property (all assets except real property)	Within or Without B.C.	Value at Death
Cash on hand		Within BC	$ 500.00
*Savings Account No. 12345 Great Savings, Downtown Branch, Vancouver, BC		Within BC	3,000.00
Policy #324-A01 with Risky Insurance, payable to Tammy Testator		Within BC	10,000.00
	TOTAL		$13,500.00

GROSS VALUE OF ESTATE	

PART III	Debts and Liabilities	Paid or Unpaid	Amount
Loan Bank — 002 Main Street		Unpaid	$ 7,000.00
**Mortgage in favor of Great West Mortgage Company			20,000.00
	TOTAL		$27,000.00

Safety Deposit Box No. 98765   Location: Safety Bank, 007 Main Street, Vancouver

PART IV   Distribution of Estate

Name and Address	Relationship	Property Passing
Tammy Thomasina Testator	Wife	Entire Estate

This is Exhibit "B" referred to in the Affidavit of

Tammy Thomasina Testator sworn before me at

Vancouver this _15th_ day of

September , 20 _0-_ .

l. M. Commissioner

A Commissioner, etc.

SELF-COUNSEL PRESS-PROBATE-BC (2-0)00

*Write to bank for amount of principal and interest as at date of death.

**Write to the mortgage company to obtain outstanding balance as at date of death.

66

No. <u>12345</u>

Registry <u>Vancouver</u>

IN THE SUPREME COURT OF BRITISH COLUMBIA

Re: The Estate of <u>Tony Thomas Testator</u>, Deceased

Praecipe

REQUIRED <u>Grant of Letters Probate with one certified court copy.</u>

Dated at <u>Vancouver</u>, this <u>15th</u> day of <u>October</u>, 20 <u>0-</u>.

Person handling estate <u>Tammy Testator</u>

Address <u>123 Wills Road, Vancouver, BC</u>

Phone number <u>555-1234</u>

SELF-COUNSEL PRESS-PROBATE – BC (5-1)00

the amount over $50 000. An estate with a gross value of $125 000 would have a filing fee of $1 350.

You are required to pay the filing fee on the *gross* value of the estate. It is particularly important that you not make any errors in calculating the filing fee because the legislation makes no provisions for refunds. This could be particularly expensive if a property that is believed to be an asset of the deceased subsequently turns out not to be (with the result that the filing fee is paid on the higher amount with no means to rectify this error).

Filing fees are not applicable to assets held in joint tenancy. This is because assets held in joint tenancy are not included in a person's estate nor affected by a person's will.

This is the opposite of the situation where assets are held in common. In this case, the interest of the deceased must be included in the disclosure statement and probate filing fees apply. In order to have bonds, real estate, cars, etc. in joint tenancy they must have the words "joint tenants" inserted (after the registered owners' name) at the time this asset is acquired or registered.

A joint tenancy means that the last surviving joint tenant receives the entire property, i.e. right of survivorship.

Be very certain about the state of your relationship with the person with whom you hold the assets as a joint tenant. If you were to have a falling out with a joint tenant, i.e. with a spouse, child, etc., that person would still own his or her respective interest in the assets and you might find it very difficult or impossible to regain 100% ownership at a later time.

Delays will no doubt be longer before an executor can obtain a grant of probate because of the greater care that will be required in order to ensure that only those assets that are owned by the deceased are included in the disclosure statement.

In addition, in order to obtain the necessary grant, in most cases it may be necessary for the personal representative to pay the filing fee from his or her own assets rather than from the estate's. Check with the financial institution where the deceased had his or her accounts to ascertain if they will allow you to issue a cheque to pay these filing fees from the deceased's account. This would allow the payment of funeral expenses (prior to probate) from the deceased's account.

Applicants must file the original Affidavit of Executor executed by the applicant along with the statement of assets, liabilities, and distribution. See the latest edition of the *Probate Guide* for more information.

g. TRANSFERRING REAL ESTATE

All real property in the sole name of the deceased must pass from the deceased to the executor or executrix before it gets to the beneficiary. The beneficiary cannot receive the real estate until the personal representative receives the Grant of Letters Probate and gives a "Form A" (Freehold Transfer Form) transferring title to the beneficiary.

In the case of property held in joint tenancy by the deceased and another person (usually the spouse), the property is transferred to the surviving joint tenant upon filing in the land title office the death certificate and a Statement as to Citizenship. The Freehold Transfer Form is not required.

If the property was owned fee simple, you must complete "Form 17" (Application for Transfer) after it has been stamped or typed on the back of the death certificate. No release is needed. All applications to register or transfer real estate must now be accompanied by a form called a Property Transfer Tax Return, which is available from the land title office.

If the transfer is to a surviving joint tenant, there is no property transfer tax payable; you just claim the exemption for a surviving joint tenant.

The transmission of real property to the personal representative is exempt from tax, but when the personal representative transfers non-exempt real property to the beneficiaries, there is a tax equivalent to 1% of the value up to $200 000 and 2% of the amount that exceeds $200 000.

If the property is worth $400 000 and there are four (non-related) beneficiaries, you may wish to have four separate transfers each signed referring to an undivided one-quarter interest. If you do so, the tax payable will be $4 000 in total (i.e., 1% on each of the transfers for $100 000). If you do only one transfer, and put all four names of the beneficiaries on one document, you must pay $6 000 in tax (i.e., 1% on the first $200 000 and 2% on the remaining $200 000).

The transfer of a family farm, recreational residence or principal residence from the estate of the deceased to a beneficiary who is a related person to the deceased is exempt from this tax. A related person is defined as a spouse, child, grandparent, grandchild, great grand-child, or the spouses of any of them.

Before any property is transferred to a beneficiary or purchaser, a search must be conducted in the land title office for the area in which the property is located. Should you decide to try it yourself, you will have to get the legal description of the property from a tax assessment notice. If you cannot find a tax assessment notice, go down to the city or municipal hall tax department and ask the clerks to help you find the correct legal description of the property. You will, of course, need the correct residential address to do this.

Once you have the correct legal description, arm yourself with paper, a pencil, and change and go to the correct land title office. If you are unsure of which office to go to, telephone the one you think most likely, give the residential address, and ask which is the correct office.

The addresses of the British Columbia land title offices are listed here.

Land Titles Branch
5th Floor, 910 Government St
Victoria, BC V8V 1X4
Tel: (250) 387-1903
Fax: (250) 387-1763

Lower Mainland Land Title Office
88 - 6 Street
New Westminster, BC V3L 5B3
Tel: (604) 660-2595
Fax: (604) 660-4064

Kamloops/Nelson Land Title Office
114 - 455 Columbia St
Kamloops, BC V2C 6K4
Tel: (250) 828-4455
Fax: (250) 371-3717

Prince George/Prince Rupert Land Title Office
Ste.#153, 1011 - 4th Ave.
Prince George, BC V2L 3H9
Tel: (250) 565-6200
Fax: (250) 565-4217

Victoria Land Title Office
850 Burdett Ave.
Victoria, BC V8W 1B4
Tel: (250) 387-6331
Fax: (250) 356-6060

Once you are in the correct office, pay the nominal search fee and take your receipt to the search counter. You may have to wait in line for quite a while. Check the office hours before you go (some may be closed by mid-afternoon). Ask the clerk to bring you the book in which your land is registered. Show him or her the tax assessment notice.

One whole page of the book will be devoted to your lot, as indicated by number. This page will show you in whose name the land is registered and the specific details of any encumbrance. Make a careful copy of all the information, as any mortgages or agreements for sale must be properly described in your disclosure statement. You may make photocopies of any documents concerning the terms of an encumbrance for a nominal fee. (Always take a pencil and paper with you.)

If you are unable to go to the office yourself, you may write a letter asking for a State of Title Certificate on the legally described lot. (Enclose $10 with your letter.) This document is a photocopy of the Certificate of Indefeasible title which has existing encumbrances noted on it.

If you hesitate to do a search yourself, you could always do what the lawyers do — hire a titles search firm to do it for you. You may find one by looking in the yellow pages of the telephone book under "Title Service." If you are in the office itself and do not wish to go through with a search, ask a clerk to point a search agent out to you. A search agent's fee for a reliable search will range from $20 to $25.

If the deceased was the registered owner of a parcel of land, then a land title office Form 17, an office copy of the disclosure statement, along with a court-certified copy of the Grant of Letters Probate or Administration from the Probate Office must be filed at the appropriate land title office. The Form 17 stamp is available at the land title office. This will enable the property, or interest in land, to be conveyed into the name of the executor, except in the case of a joint tenancy which is discussed above.

The executor's status should appear on all documents of the land title office as, for example, "John Doe, executor of the estate of James Doe, deceased," and the address should be inserted.

When such a conveyance is to be made to an executor or administrator, it is recommended that it be done in consultation with a lawyer because there are many legal details and requirements involved in transferring real property.

If it looks like it will take a long time to process an estate and there is an extra car or truck which no one will be able to use, it may be a good idea to see if you can transfer and sell the asset immediately in order to avoid the loss caused by extensive depreciation.

A transfer can be done immediately if a lawyer gives an undertaking to forward the releases and a copy of the Grant of Probate to the motor vehicle registry immediately after receiving them.

Not all lawyers are aware of their ability to do this, so you may have to have them contact the motor vehicle registry to convince them to do this for you.

h. RELATIONSHIP BETWEEN EXECUTORS AND TRUSTEES

The executor or executrix is the person who is responsible for probating the estate and distributing the assets to the beneficiaries. A trustee, on the other hand, is the person who administers a trust agreement. A trust agreement does not necessarily arise out of an estate although commonly an estate is involved.

An executor's position is temporary, perhaps lasting a year until the estate is settled, but a trustee's may carry on for many years, depending on the terms of the trust. A trustee should definitely be a person with experience in business affairs.

Finally, as both persons are involved with personal confidences, they should be closely related to the person making the will and the beneficiaries. Often one person will fill both positions.

i. FEES OF EXECUTORS, TRUSTEES, AND LAWYERS

If you handle any of the work and responsibilities of probate alone or in conjunction with a lawyer, you should be careful to keep an accurate account of all the work done and of any money expended in connection with the work that you perform in case it is necessary to justify the expenses to the other beneficiaries.

Executors and/or trustees may charge up to 5% of the gross aggregate value of the estate *and* 5% of income (interest on the estate) for their work. Gross aggregate value equals total value *before* deducting debts. As you can see, this can be quite expensive. This "5-plus-5" formula is almost always used by trust companies.

The fee which may be charged by executors is granted them as a group and it is up to them to decide how to divide it among themselves. If they are unable to do so, they can apply to the courts for an apportionment.

If there is a compensation agreement between the executor and the deceased, then the standard fee may be varied either up or down. If the executor is also a legatee or a beneficiary, the general rule is that the benefit is granted instead of compensation for work as executor. This presumption may be overcome by inserting a specific clause permitting the executor or executrix to have his or her fee (e.g., "The gift to Ernie Executor is in addition to and not in substitution for his remuneration as executor").

A person who has a choice between receiving money as personal representative or as a beneficiary is often better off to receive it as a beneficiary. Payment for services as an executor are included in income, and as such, are taxable.

Lawyers may charge up to 2% of the gross value on average size ($100 000) estates for handling the probate, while large estates are normally charged around 1% of the gross value. A lawyer who is also the executor or trustee cannot take both fees unless the will expressly states that, so he or she must elect which to take. Trustees are often executors as well and usually charge 5% of the value of the gross estate. The total is 5% regardless of how it is apportioned in their role as executors and trustees and regardless of the number of executors and trustees.

The following should be considered in determining fees.

(a) How large is the estate?

(b) How much work has had to be done?

(c) How much time has had to be spent?

(d) What ability has the trustee shown?

(e) Has the trustee increased the value of the estate or not?

j. WHAT TO DO IF YOU CONSIDER YOUR LEGAL BILL TOO HIGH

If the beneficiaries feel that the legal fees or the trustees' fees are too high, they may have the bill taxed by visiting their nearest court registry and referring the matter to the district registrar. He or she will then set an appointment where the lawyer, the beneficiaries, and the registrar will go over the bill. Following this examination, the registrar will make a decision. The clerks in the court registry (probate division or otherwise) are very helpful if further information or assistance is required.

4

ADMINISTRATION

If you have properly completed a will, you need not be concerned with this chapter, but if you are involved in the administration of an estate or have not yet made your will, the following information will be of interest to you.

a. WHO CAN CLAIM?

The Estate Administration Act provides that if a person dies without a will and leaves a common-law spouse, the spouse may apply to the court for a share of the estate as the court directs, provided he or she lived with the deceased and was being supported by the deceased for a minimum of two years immediately preceding the death. Common-law spouses must make the claim against the estate within six months from the date of the Grant of Administration.

The "rights" of a common-law spouse are, at the present time, unclear and it will be up to the courts to sort out the division of property between the competing interests of the legal and common-law spouses if both survive the deceased.

The act also says that where the deceased leaves a spouse (including common-law) or children, then no application may be made to the court without service of notice on the spouse or children.

As a general statement, the problems of dealing with an estate as an administrator are considerably more complicated than as an executor. Basically, an application must be made to the court on behalf of the administrator. In addition, several other applications and actual appearances in court may have to be made; the consents of the various bene-ficiaries concerned must be obtained; and the administrator may be required to post a bond. The administration of an estate involves more paperwork and is more complicated, costly, and time-consuming than an executorship. Therefore, it is strongly recommended that you consult a lawyer if you are in this situation. Don't attempt to handle the details alone.

b. DISTRIBUTION

If the deceased left no will, his or her survivors would share the assets of the estate in accordance with the following priorities. Note that the surviving spouse receives all of the household furnishings as well as a life estate in the matri-monial home for as long as he or she wishes to remain there.

1. An unmarried man or woman

If a person who has not been married dies without a will, the entire estate can be distributed equally among the next-of-kin in the class or degree closest in blood relationship.

There are a number of different degrees or classes of beneficiaries. If only one heir is living in the closest blood relation class, he or she is entitled to the entire estate; none of the relations in the subsequent classes receives any benefit from the estate of the deceased. If the deceased's mother and father are alive, the estate will go to them.

2. A widower or widow without issue

Where a widower or widow dies without a will or without issue, his or her entire estate is distributed as set forth in the distribution schedule for an unmarried man or woman.

3. A widower or widow with issue

(a) If a widower or widow dies without a will, leaving one child surviving, the child receives the entire estate.

(b) If a widower or widow dies without a will, leaving more than one child surviving, the entire estate is divided among those children.

(c) The child(ren) of any deceased child in either (a) or (b) receives the share which the deceased child would have received if living.

4. A married man without issue

If a married man dies without a will and his widow survives him but there are no issue, the entire estate goes to the widow absolutely.

5. A married woman without issue

If a married woman dies without a will and her widower survives her but there are no issue, the entire estate goes to the widower absolutely.

6. A married man with issue

(a) If a married man dies without a will, leaving a widow and one child surviving him, and his estate does not exceed $65 000, his entire estate goes to his widow.

If this estate exceeds $65 000, the first $65 000 goes to his widow and the residue of his estate is divided equally between the widow and the child.

(b) If a married man dies without a will, leaving a widow and more than one child surviving him, and his estate does not exceed $65 000, his entire estate goes to his widow.

If his estate exceeds $65 000, the first $65 000 goes to his widow, and the residue of his estate is divided so that one third goes to the widow and two-thirds are divided equally among the children.

If there are two or more children, they all get an equal portion of the two-thirds that remain of the residue of the estate, after the widow has taken her $65 000 and one-third portion of the estate.

(c) Any child or children of a deceased child would be entitled to the share which the parent would have received if living by virtue of the division under paragraphs (a) and (b) above.

7. A married woman with issue

(a) If a married woman dies without a will, leaving a widower and one child surviving her, and her estate does not exceed $65 000, her entire estate goes to her widower.

   If her estate exceeds $65 000, the first $65 000 goes to her widower and the residue of her estate is divided equally between the widower and the child.

(b) If a married woman dies without a will, leaving a widower and more than one child surviving her, and her estate does not exceed $65 000, her entire estate goes to her widower.

   If her estate exceeds $65 000 the first $65 000 goes to her widower and the residue of her estate is divided, one-third to the widower and two-thirds equally between the children (see 6(b) if more than two children).

(c) Any child or children of a deceased child would be entitled to the share which the parent would have received if living by virtue of the division under paragraphs (a) and (b).

8. Distribution schedule

The following are the degrees of classes and their priority as claimants on the estate of the deceased.

(a) Wife or husband, and issue, if any, as above

(b) Father and mother, or survivor

(c) Brothers and sisters, and children of deceased brothers and sisters per stirpes (see Glossary for definition)

(d) Nephews and nieces equally

(e) Other degrees of relationship determined through the nearest common ancestor

c. WHO MAY APPLY FOR ADMINISTRATION?

Generally, only one person applies for Letters of Administration if there is no will. The court has the discretion of granting Letters of Administration to people (or to a person) other than those normally entitled to share in the estate.

If a next-of-kin refuses to consent to the granting of Letters of Administration, then the administrator may be required to post a bond.

If an executor refuses to act, or renounces his or her office, and has no authorization to substitute another executor then the estate is in the same position as if there had been no executor appointed. The court will then appoint an administrator who must follow the directions of the will. The application in this situation is for a Grant of Letters of Administration with Will Annexed.

d. WHAT IF CHILDREN ARE INVOLVED?

In a situation where there is no will and there are infant children, the distribution of the estate is delayed further because the public administrator or the public trustee's office in Vancouver must consent to the appointment of the administrator. Usually no objection is raised if it is the surviving spouse and there has not been a divorce or judicial separation.

The consent of the public administrator or the public trustee's office is always required when the property of children is being dealt with. A bond is usually required up to the amount of their interest before the court will confirm the appointment of the surviving spouse or any other individual as the administrator. If the amount of the bond required for such an administrator is $70 000, the premium would be approximately $270 per year. Bondspeople are listed in the yellow pages under "Bonds and Sureties."

Because of their age, infant children may not enforce their rights against the estate in their own name. The public trustee protects their rights. Consequently, the monies are either used by the surviving spouse or placed in the court to the credit of the children until they reach 19 years. At that time the amount placed in the court, together with interest compounding at the rate of 1% per year below the banks' prime commercial lending rate (i.e., if bank rate is 11%, the rate paid is 10%) is paid to them. If the money was used by the surviving spouse, the children may claim the full share on reaching age 19.

If the amount is used by the family or by the surviving spouse, then an accounting must be maintained. (All monies and transactions involving the money of the children must be accounted for at the end of two years from the beginning of the time at which the monies were being utilized. At the end of each two-year period a reconciliation of the trust monies must be made by a certified general accountant or by a chartered accountant.)

If there is a will, however, the problems of posting a bond will not be present as the executor has full ownership of all assets of the property without the requirement of any bond — so make a will!

5

TRUSTS AND TRUSTEES

When infants, invalids, or immature individuals are beneficiaries, you may wish to appoint a trustee to handle their
assets until such time as they are able to manage their own
affairs. Following is a brief introduction to trusts.

a. WHAT IS A TRUSTEE?

A trustee may be an individual or a corporate entity, such as
a trust company. Trustees are given the power in a will to
exercise many functions, including taking in money, invest-
ing money, selling assets, and distributing the proceeds of an
estate in accordance with the terms of the trust that has been
established.

Usually a trustee is involved when, for example, you
either do not wish to give a lump sum gift to an individual
whom you suspect may squander the money, or you wish to
have a more capable manager than the beneficiary handle the
affairs of the estate.

Usually, the beneficiary receives set monthly or bimonthly
payments from the trust of an amount adequate to pay living
expenses as they arise. Trust funds may also be created to
handle the affairs of an estate for the benefit of infants (anyone
who has not attained the age of 19). In these cases, payments
are generally made to parents or guardians for the maintenance and education of the child. A trust in favor of a surviving
spouse may contain the proviso that payments shall be received as long as he or she does not remarry.

Three other common trust arrangements are for the following:

(a) Invalids (for whom payments may be made directly to the private hospital or nursing home to which they are confined)

(b) Charitable organizations (such as the United Way)

(c) Educational establishments (such as universities)

A common provision in a trust directs that the interest from the trust fund be paid to a named individual or organization, while the principal amount of the estate stays invested in the trust fund to earn more interest. Also, it is common to include a provision that, upon the occurrence of a stated event, for example, an infant reaching the age of 19, the principal amount or "corpus" of the trust fund is to be paid to the beneficiary.

If you plan to create a trust, you must bear in mind that trustees will have control of the estate's assets for a much longer period than executors would. Therefore, it is very important that the trustee be younger than you and that there be an alternative trustee in case one refuses to act, or dies before you do. Always get the prior consent of the persons you wish to name as trustees and their assurance that, if named, they will act.

If a trustee refuses to act, the trust may be put into the hands of the public administrator who, as a civil servant having many other responsibilities, may not have the time to give the estate the attention it would require.

b. THE TRUSTEE ACT (British Columbia)

This act, while it does not excuse or release a prior appointed trustee from liability, does permit a new trustee to be appointed if —

(a) a trustee dies,

(b) he or she is outside of British Columbia for more than 12 months,

(c) he or she wants to retire,

(d) he or she refuses to act, or

(e) he or she is incapable of acting.

An executor or trustee has limited powers to delegate authority to others or to employ agents. In fact, at common law, the delegation of power is usually prohibited. However, this does not apply where —

(a) a person acting on his or her own account would, in a similar situation, hire an agent, for example, a real estate agent, or

(b) trust business has to be transacted outside the jurisdiction of the court that confirmed the appointment of the trustee and/or executor.

c. A TRUST COMPANY AS A TRUSTEE?

If you are considering setting up a trust, you should consult a lawyer, especially if the amount involved is substantial. You may even wish to consider appointing a trust company as trustee. The main advantage of a trust company is that, unlike an individual trustee, it never dies. On the other hand, very large trust companies may have a tendency to become impersonal and expensive, so seek out a trust company that offers you prompt personal service and assistance.

Note that wills drawn by some trust companies sometimes include a clause that releases the trust company from any liability for any act or acts, even if the estate suffers losses as a result of such act or acts.

However, case law suggests that this "release" clause does not protect the trust company because it must act in the same manner as a prudent person would when administering a trust.

The usual fee charged by trust companies for acting as executors and trustees is 5% of the income and assets of the estate. The charge on income is sometimes called a management fee and the trust company may charge more if there is an express management contract for a higher percentage. You can easily see that if the estate is a large one, the management fee could amount to a considerable yearly sum. Note also that the executor's fees are based on the gross value of the estate. In other words, if the estate is valued at $200 000, but has liabilities of $150 000, the 5% is based on the $200 000 (i.e., $10 000 and not on the net worth of $50 000).

d. CONDITIONAL TRUSTS

If you establish a trust, the funds or assets within the trust no longer form part of your estate that can be dealt with by a will. If you establish this trust during your lifetime, it is called an "inter vivos trust." A testamentary trust is one that is included within your will.

Once a trust has been established, the trustee is bound by its provisions. The beneficiaries under the trust, if the gifts are conditional, must wait until the condition has been fulfilled before receiving their benefit. An example of a conditional benefit conferred within a trust might be as follows:

> To my daughter, Stella Smith, I give one-third of the capital and income contained in this trust on the express condition that she receives it only if she graduates from an accredited university.

In this case, unless the daughter graduated from university, she would not be entitled to the money.

If there are children involved in a trust, the question often arises as to whether or not they may receive their share of the trust assets as soon as they reach the age of majority (19). If a trust is set up, for example, so that the children would each receive one-third of their total share in the trust at specified time periods (e.g., only if they reach 25, 30, and 35 years of age), then they would receive it at those ages.

In cases where the wording of the trust has been careless, it may be possible for the children who are named within the trust to apply to receive their portions of the trust at the age of majority. Had the trust specified that they would receive their share of the trust ONLY IF they attained the ages of 25, 30, and 35, then it may well be that they would be prohibited from receiving their share until they reached those respective ages. Alternately, a clause granting a bequest only if the beneficiary fulfils a condition before receiving the bequest may be used.

As this area of the law is very complex and has an infinite number of variables it is suggested that whenever dealing with a trust or a benefit under a trust that a lawyer should be consulted.

6

BENEFITS AVAILABLE FROM THE CANADA PENSION PLAN

If a deceased person had contributed to the Canada Pension Plan (which is required by most people while earning income from their employment) for at least three calendar years, then his or her survivors may obtain certain benefits. These benefits can be broken down into four categories:

(a) A death benefit is payable to the estate in a lump sum. This is to be used to help defray immediate expenses such as funeral and ambulance costs.

(b) The surviving spouse may be entitled to a monthly pension.

(c) The surviving dependent children may be entitled to a monthly pension.

(d) A disabled spouse of a deceased person who can show that he or she relied completely or to a large degree on his or her spouse for maintenance (financial support) may qualify for a monthly pension.

The lump sum benefit referred to in (a) has a maximum value of $2 500.

For further details on the actual amount and application forms, you should contact the branch of the Canada Pension office closest to you or call 1-800-277-9914.

The death benefit form must be completed and returned to the Canada Pension department together with —

(a) the death certificate,

(b) the deceased's birth certificate,

(c) the deceased's social insurance card or number, and

(d) the T-4 slips for years he or she contributed (last three years will do) or the form called a "Statement of Contributory Salary and Wages."

a. SURVIVING SPOUSE'S PENSION

The amount of this pension depends on the amount of the deceased's contributions during his or her lifetime. The amount of the pension will be calculated for you when you supply the Canada Pension department with —

(a) the death certificate,

(b) the deceased's birth certificate,

(c) the deceased's social insurance card or number,

(d) the marriage certificate,

(e) the spouse's birth certificate,

(f) the spouse's social insurance number, and

(g) the deceased's T-4 slips or Statement of Contributory Salary and Wages.

It is interesting to note that the surviving spouse's pension no longer ceases upon remarriage. In addition, if the new marriage ends in death, the original surviving spouse then has the right to claim either the first pension or the second, if higher.

1. The common-law spouse

To be eligible for death benefits, the common-law spouse need only show that the couple had resided together for at least one year as husband and wife, and that the deceased had publicly represented the applicant as his or her spouse. The Minister of Health and Welfare Canada has the same discretion to direct that the survivor be considered the spouse of the deceased for Canada Pension Plan purposes.

If the discretion is exercised in favor of a common-law spouse, the normal application can be made by the survivor for the benefits that are available under the plan, as if the survivor and the deceased contributor had actually been married.

If you find yourself in such a situation, you should immediately contact your local office of the Canada Pension Plan (which you can find in the telephone directory) and discuss the facts of your particular situation with the proper officials.

b. CANADA PENSION PLAN CHILDREN'S BENEFIT

The benefit for surviving children is paid to the natural or adopted child(ren) of the deceased contributor or a child in the care and control of the deceased contributor at the time of death. The child must be under 18 or between 18 and 25 and attending school, (full-time) at a recognized institution. Until a child reaches 18 the benefits are paid to the parent or guardian. They continue as long as the criteria set out above are followed.

The survivor's pension application form and related documents, together with the child's birth certificate and social insurance number or card, are needed to complete the application.

Complete information booklets on how to file the various applications are available from your nearest Canada Pension office.

One provision is of particular importance to estates. In some cases, a person would have been entitled to a CPP disability or retirement pension in his or her own right or to a survivor's benefit (on the death of a contributing spouse), but died without applying for the benefit. In these cases, the estate, representative, or heir of that person or a designated person or agency may apply for and receive the retroactive benefit to which the deceased person would have been enti-tled, up to a maximum of one year's benefit. The application must be made within one year of the death of the person.

This same provision applies where the child of a deceased or a disabled contributor dies before reaching age 18 and before an application for benefit is made. In this case, how-ever, the person having custody and control of the child at death may apply for the benefit.

APPENDIX 1
PROBATE CHECKLIST

Following is a point-by-point checklist of things to do in probating an estate and taking care of the affairs of the deceased.

Date Completed

1. Locate the will. _____

2. Apply for a death certificate. _____

3. Apply for a wills search. _____

4. Check the safety deposit box. _____

5. Publish a notice to creditors (not mandatory). _____

6. Make an inventory of assets and debts. _____

7. Obtain available cash. _____

8. Send in change of address form to post office. _____

9. Notify old age pension offices (federal and provincial). _____

10. Cancel subscriptions, charge accounts, etc. _____

11. File or calculate income tax payable by deceased for the year of death. _____

12. Fill out statement of assets and liabilities. _____

13. Make out Affidavit of Executor. _____

14. Make out a Section 135(6) Affidavit. _____

15. Make out the Notice of
    Application.   _____

16. Make out the Praecipe.   _____

17. Make out Declaration of
    Citizenship (if applicable).   _____

18. Have documents in steps 12, 13,
    14, 15, and 17 sworn.   _____

19. Mail the Notice of Application.   _____

20. File the documents in steps 12, 13,
    14, 15, and 16 at the court
    registry (probate division).   _____

21. File tax return for the estate
    if applicable.   _____

22. Transfer titles to the property.   _____

23. Transfer insurance on house,
    car, etc.   _____

24. File claims for life and other
    insurance.   _____

25. Pay accounts outstanding and
    legal and administration fees.   _____

26. Apply for Canada Pension Plan
    death benefits.   _____

27. Apply for civil service, union,
    and/or veterans' benefits.   _____

28. Distribute balance of cash
    according to the will (reserving
    enough cash to pay income tax
    for deceased and estate if not
    already paid).   _____

There can be no probate or administration until seven
days after death. This gives the executor or administrator an
opportunity to find all the relevant documents.

APPENDIX 2
ADDRESSES

If you would like more information about the BC Transplant Society and/or its research activities, or would like to make a donation to the Foundation please write, you can contact them at:

BC TRANSPLANT SOCIETY

3rd Floor, West Tower
555 West 12th Ave
Vancouver, B.C.
V5Z 3X7
Tel: 604-877-2100
Toll free: 1-800-663-6189
Fax: 604-877-2111
Email: webmaster@bcts.hnet.bc.ca

Their web site (English and Chinese) can be found at:
http://www.transplant.bc.ca/

VITAL STATISTICS AGENCY

GENERAL INQUIRIES
Vancouver area: 660-2937

Victoria area: 952-2681
Elsewhere: 1-800-663-8328 or by
Fax at (250) 952-2182
on the Web at: http://www.hlth.gov.bc.ca/vs/index.html

VICTORIA
818 Fort Street
Phone: (250) 952-2681
Fax: (250) 952-2527

VANCOUVER
605 Robson Street, Room 250
Phone:(604) 660-2937
Fax: (604) 660-2645

KELOWNA
101, 1475 Ellis Street
Phone: (250) 712-7562
Fax: (250) 712-7598

PRINCE GEORGE
433 Queensway
Phone: (250) 565-7105
Fax: (250) 565-7106

GLOSSARY

ADMINISTRATOR

Individual appointed by the court to administer the estate of a person who dies without a will (feminine form is "administratrix")

AFFIDAVIT

A sworn statement in writing, made before an authorized officer

ASSETS

Property of a deceased person subject by law to payment of his or her debts and legacies

BENEFICIARY

Name given to a person who receives some benefit, whether money or property, from the will of a deceased person

CAPITAL GAIN

Profit earned on the sale of an asset or profit deemed to be realized on the death of an individual, as if the asset had been sold on the date of death

CAPITAL LOSS

Loss experienced on the sale of an asset or loss deemed to be experienced on the death of an individual, as if the asset had been sold on the date of death

CODICIL

Change or addition to a will requiring all the formalities of signing and witnessing needed for a will

COMMISSIONER FOR TAKING OATHS

An official appointed by law to take affidavits

CREDITOR

Person to whom money is due

DEVOLVE

Pass by transmission or succession

DISCLOSURE STATEMENT

A document filed by the executor or administrator with the probate fees department

ENCROACH

Act of paying out or spending portions of the money or other assets being held as a trust fund

ESCHEAT

Process by which the assets of a deceased pass to the provincial government when he or she dies without a will and without a spouse or next-of-kin

ESTATE

The degree, quality, nature, and extent of a person's interest in, or ownership of, land or other property treated like land

ESTATE ADMINISTRATION ACT

The British Columbia statute providing for the distribution of the estate of an individual who dies without a will

EXECUTOR

Individual appointed in a will to administer the estate of the deceased (feminine form is "executrix")

HOLOGRAPH WILL

Will written completely in the handwriting of the person making it, having no witnesses to the signature of that person, generally not valid for residents of British Columbia

INTESTATE

Either the act of dying without a will or the person who dies without a will

LETTERS OF ADMINISTRATION

Court grant appointing an administrator to administer the estate of an individual who dies without a will

LETTERS OF ADMINISTRATION WITH WILL ANNEXED

Court grant appointing an administrator to administer the estate of an individual who left a will, where the named executor has died or is unable or unwilling to act

LETTERS PROBATE

Court grant confirming the appointment of an executor named in a will and confirming the validity of the will itself

LIFE INTEREST

Benefit given to a beneficiary in a will which permits that beneficiary to have the use of some property or some amount of money for the balance of the beneficiary's lifetime only

NEXT-OF-KIN

Blood relatives of a person who dies without a will who inherit by reason of the Estate Administration Act

NOTARIAL COPY

True copy of an original document certified by a lawyer or notary public as being a true copy

OATH

Solemn affirmation of the truth of what is stated

PERSONAL PROPERTY

All property with the exception of real estate and buildings (also known as "personalty")

PERSONAL REPRESENTATIVE

Name given to the individual administering an estate, whether he or she be an executor/executrix or admini-strator/administratrix

PER STIRPES

Method of dividing assets of an estate so that if a member of the group among which the assets are being divided is dead at the time of the division, the children of that deceased member of the group will divide among them the share that their parent would have received had he or she been alive

POWER OF ATTORNEY

A written document by which you grant to someone the authority to act on your behalf on various matters. A power of attorney is different from a will, which provides for the orderly distribution of your estate after your death; a power of attorney terminates on your death

PRECEDENT

Guide or example which has been used before

PROBATE DIVISION OF THE SUPREME COURT

Court responsible for the appointment of personal repre-sentatives and generally involved with problems arising dur-ing the administration of estates

REAL PROPERTY

Land and buildings (also known as "real estate" and "realty")

RESIDUARY BENEFICIARY
Beneficiary to whom the residue of the estate is left

RESIDUE
That portion of an estate remaining after all specific bequests and specific devises have been made

SPECIFIC BEQUEST
Gift under a will of a specific item of personal property or a specific amount of cash

SPECIFIC DEVISE
Gift under a will of a specific item of real property

TESTATE
Either the act of dying with a will or a person who dies leaving a will

TESTATOR
Individual who makes a will (feminine form is "testatrix")

TRANSFER
Act of conveying the title to property

TRANSMISSION
Act of conveying the title to property where the rights of the beneficiary take effect on the death of the donor

WILLS VARIATION ACT
The British Columbia statute permitting a spouse or dependent child to obtain benefits from the estate of a deceased if not adequately provided for by the will